This book is
the last

D0833618

5· 11 · 10

Stuff that scares your PANTS off!

Glenn Murphy received his masters in science communication from London's Imperial College of Science, Technology and Medicine. He wrote his first popular science book, *Why Is Snot Green?*, while working at the Science Museum in London. In 2007 he moved to the United States. He now lives and works in Raleigh, North Carolina, with his wife, Heather, and an increasingly large and ill-tempered cat.

Why Is Snot Green? was shortlisted for the Blue Peter Book Awards 2007, Best Book with Facts category, and the Royal Society Prize for Science Books Junior Prize 2008.

Stuff that scares your PANTS off!

The Science Museum Book of
Scary Things (and ways to avoid them)

Glenn Murphy

Illustrated by Mike Phillips

MACMILLAN CHILDREN'S BOOKS

First published 2009 by Macmillan Children's Books
a division of Macmillan Publishers Limited
20 New Wharf Road, London N1 9RR
Basingstoke and Oxford
Associated companies throughout the world
www.panmacmillan.com

ISBN 978-0-330-51227-5

1 3 5 7 9 8 6 4 2

A CIP catalogue record for this book is available from
the British Library.

Typeset by Nigel Hazle
Printed and bound in the UK by CPI Mackays, Chatham ME5 8TD

To Damon, Debs and Gaby –
for being fearless in the face of risky book ideas

Thanks to:

Damon McCollin-Moore, Deborah Bloxam, Fran Bate, Sarah Richardson, Katie Maggs, Rob Skitmore and everyone at the Science Museum who offered their ideas and comments

Gaby Morgan and everyone at Macmillan Children's Books, for continuing transatlantic support

Dr Annabel Price

Julia Hewlett and Professor Alun Williams from the Royal Veterinary College

Jane, Omar, Brad and Victoria – for putting me up (and putting up with me) during the summer book tour in London – the Mitcham Massive lives on

The Schwichows, the Sherrills, the Fab Four (well, the other three) and all our new friends in NC

The Witts and the Murphs

and, as always, Heather and the Fuzzball – couldn't do this without you.

Contents

Introduction

Shark attacks. Plane crashes. Deadly diseases. Ghosts, monsters and aliens. This book is jam-packed with bad, scary stuff, and covers just about anything that you could possibly be afraid of.

But this is more than a big book of 'bad' and 'scary'. It's a journey into fear itself.

Along the way, we'll travel deep into the unknown territories of the mind and body, searching for the roots and workings of fear, phobia and panic.

We'll look at what fears are, where they come from, and how to work with them, live with them, and get around them. We'll explore the wide world of things that make people afraid, and weigh up how scary they really are. We'll look at the chances of the bad stuff really happening, and we'll give you the lowdown on how to avoid it.

From earthquakes and hurricanes to spiders and snakes; from doctors and dentists to planes, trains and car crashes; from darkness and drowning to ghosts and the Great Beyond – we'll face every terror in our quest for understanding. With a bit of biology, a spot of psychology, and oodles of lovely facts and figures, we'll learn everything there is to know about our fears. We'll see how they begin, how they build and balloon into phobias, and how we can use our new knowledge to stop fear and panic in their tracks.

Sound good to you? Or scary, perhaps? How about both?

Good and scary – that's a great way to begin. So let's get going!

1 Wild and Scary Wildlife

The Fears You're Born With and the Fears You Learn

Some people scream at the sight of snakes and spiders. Others keep huge ones as pets, and let them slither or scuttle all over them while they watch TV. Hardly anyone, however, would be happy to see a tiger or bear charging at them through a forest. And anyone who giggles underwater bubbles at the razor-filled maw of a shark clearly has something wrong with them.* There are some fears, it seems, that some folks can 'switch off', while others mean 'new underpants, please' for almost everybody.

So how does this come about? Are you just *born* afraid

---

* Or, perhaps, laughing gas in their scuba tank.

of certain things like sharks, snakes and spiders? Or are you born fearless, and only later learn to be afraid as you grow up and experience scary things for yourself?

The answer is, it's actually a little of both.

Humans and other animals seem to be born with some fears, which we call inborn (or *innate*) fears. These include the dark, loud noises and sudden movements. Some animals are also born with the fear of a specific predator. Mice, for example, are born fearing cats and foxes, which makes perfect sense, if you think about it. Mice born without a fear of the things that hunt them probably don't survive long in the wild. So the foolishly fearless mice have been weeded out and killed off (an example of *natural selection*), leaving only cat-and-fox-phobic mice behind to survive and thrive.

Similarly, many of the things humans are commonly scared of seem connected to our survival as a species. A healthy fear of thunder and lightning probably helped keep our ancestors alive during thunderstorms, as the crack and boom sent them running for cover. (Once there, they were less likely to find themselves caught out in the open – as the tallest, most zappable objects around – see page 56.) Likewise, a healthy fear of large predators (like bears and tigers) or potentially poisonous animals (like snakes and spiders) would surely have helped them survive in the wild too.

Our brains haven't evolved that much in the last 10,000 years. In fact, they're largely the same now as they were in our Stone Age ancestors. This helps explain why people living in modern cities would still be so scared of tigers and snakes, even though most of them have never even seen them outside of zoos, much less been attacked by them. In a way, our brains are wired or preprogrammed to fear' prehistoric threats, not modern ones like fast cars and fast food.

But that can't be the whole story either. Otherwise, everyone would be born afraid of the same things, and no one would be afraid of more 'modern' things like aeroplanes and lifts, when clearly some people are. Nor would it explain rarer phobias of seemingly harmless things, like *dendrophobia*, the fear of trees, or *alektorophobia*, the devastating fear of chickens.*

In fact, beyond a few, universal fears – like the dark, loud noises and sudden movements – most human fears are either completely learned from experience, or are developed into full-blown fears from *predispositions* (or fear 'leanings') that we're born with. So instead of being born *totally* afraid of snakes, spiders or bears, you're actually born afraid of certain shapes and types of movement. Then how you react to each animal depends on what you experience, and what you see and learn from those around you.

Here's how it works. Young monkeys, apes and human children can all instantly recognize the linear, slithering motion of a snake. But how they react to it depends on whether or not the snake bites them, and how others

---

* Even, believe it or not, frozen and cooked ones.

around them react when they see one. If the snake bites, or someone around the baby freaks out, then the youngster is afraid for life. If not, they'll think of snakes as harmless until shown otherwise. Similarly, a charging bear or tiger makes a huge, fast-moving shape which will startle anyone. But children don't learn to fear bears and tigers specifically until they're attacked by one or (much more often) told that they attack people.*

And right there is the key to putting the fear of a dangerous animal in its proper place. Often we develop the fear of an animal because we're *told* it's dangerous, because we've heard a scary story about one, or because we've seen the frightened reactions to animals of our parents and friends as we grow up.

Many wild animals, to be sure, should never be messed with. But that doesn't mean they're necessarily looking to *mess with us*. Compared to the other dangers of modern life, very few people are ever harmed or killed by wild animals. If you understand that – plus a little about animal behaviour – then you need never be terrified of an animal again.

Even the dreaded evil chicken.

---

* Think about it – ever hear the story *Goldilocks and the Three Bears* when you were little? A nasty slur on porridge-loving bears everywhere, that one . . .

A naval nightmare

On 30 July 1945, the US Navy cruiser USS *Indianapolis* was sunk by a Japanese submarine, near the island of Guam in the Philippine Sea. Of the 1,200 sailors on board, around 300 died in the attack, while just under 900 managed to jump overboard, with or without life vests.

By sunrise the next day, the first sharks appeared.

At first they simply circled the survivors, who clung to each other to stay afloat. By day two, there were hundreds of sharks circling all around, and the desperate sailors, sunburned, thirsty and exhausted, gave up any hope of rescue. Where before they shouted for help, now they fell into an awful silence.

From day three onwards, the silence was broken every few minutes by a strangled scream as the sharks began to pick off the survivors, one by one. When a rescue boat finally arrived on day five, the captain watched horrified as the sharks continued to attack the men he was struggling to pull from the water.

In the end, only 317 men survived. In the worst known attack on record, a swarm of frenzied oceanic White-Tip Sharks took most of the rest.

The fear

Eaten by a man-eating shark. Yikes! You don't get much scarier than that. Sharks have evolved over millions of years into perfect underwater killing machines. At one end, a mouthful of razor blades; at the other, a powerful tail which drives it through the water like a grinning torpedo . . . headed straight towards you and your flailing legs. Sharks can smell a drop of blood in a million gallons of water. They can sense the electricity in your twitching muscles. And above all – they play the cello as they eat you. Daaaaa-dum, daaaaa-dum, dum-dum-dum-dumm-daaa-dum . . .

The reality

Right? Well, not quite. Although some sharks are quite definitely dangerous animals, many are completely harmless to humans. Honest! Even the so-called 'maneaters', like Great White Sharks, are not the bloodthirsty killers that movie directors would have us believe. And trust me, none of them can play stringed instruments. At all.

There are over 350 known species of shark. Of those,

only a few – such as Great Whites, Reef Sharks and Tiger Sharks – pose any threat to humans. And while it's true that these sharks *do* occasionally attack swimmers and divers, it's almost always by mistake. Most attacks happen to divers who try to feed or prod sharks (not very bright) or surfers who fall off their boards and on to sharks, surprising them (just plain unlucky). Unprovoked shark attacks also happen, but usually to swimmers and surfers who, to a shark, happen to look a lot like seals or turtles from below – a painful but honest mistake. In any case, once a shark has taken a bite out of a human it usually lets go and swims off rather than sticking around to chew and swallow.

Now, I know what you might be thinking. 'Great – when I'm lying on the beach with my legs bitten off, I'll feel a *lot* better knowing that the poor shark didn't do it on purpose.' But if you think about it, the idea that sharks really *want* to eat us is half the reason we're afraid of them. The other half, of course, is that they *can* and *do* eat us. Like, all the time. But do they?

The chances

According to the *International Shark Attack File* – a record of shark attacks kept by biologists worldwide – the average number of shark attacks per year worldwide is about 50. About 15 per year happen in Florida, USA, with the rest split between Australia (6 per year), Brazil (5 per year), South Africa (4 per year) and other regions. So how many of those attacks turn out to be deadly? Well, the average number of shark-attack deaths each year in Florida is zero. Yep – fifteen bites, no deaths. In other regions (where it takes longer to get from the beach to a hospital) the average might go as high as one death per year.

Just one. Now nobody wants to *be that one,* of course. But if you compare your chances of dying in a shark attack to dying of something else, it helps put our whole fear of deadly sharks into place.

Let's take a quick look at some numbers.

About 1,638 shark attacks happened worldwide between 1960 and 2007. Of these, about 40% (around 650 attacks) happened in the United States, which – as we've already seen – seems to be a particularly popular place for sharks to dine on us.

But the victim was actually killed in less than 1% of these attacks. In fact, fewer than 20 people have died from shark attacks in American waters in the last 100 years. That's just one person every five years, despite the fact that millions of people swim in the waters off Florida and California every year.

One of the years when someone did die from an unprovoked* shark attack was 2003. One person dead, out of about 40 recorded shark bites in the USA that year. Now compare that with some of the other causes of deaths in the USA during the same year:

---

* We won't bother mentioning the *provoked* ones. Seriously, if you actually go about *provoking* sharks, you probably deserve whatever toothy response is coming to you.

Total number of deaths in 2003	2,448,288
Heart disease, cancer and strokes	1,399,680
Influenza and pneumonia	65,163
Motor-vehicle accidents	43,354
Firearms	28,664
Falls	13,322
Poisoning	12,757
Drowning	3,842
Other accidents	1,510
Shark attacks	1

Not the happiest picture in the world, perhaps. But at least it tells us that of all the things Americans could be worrying about, shark attacks don't come very high on the list.

The lowdown

So now we know a few things. We know that most species of shark don't attack people, and even those that *do* bite humans usually do so by mistake. We also know that even if you *are* bitten, your chances of survival are still good, as most shark attacks don't prove deadly. And in the bigger picture, shark attacks kill very, very few people when compared to other dangers.

On the other hand, no one really wants to get bitten by a shark. While it might not kill you, it's pretty much guaranteed not to be a fun experience. So what's the best way to avoid them? Well, all you really have to do is avoid beaches where sharks often like to hunt, and avoid being mistaken for a fish, seal, or turtle. To do that:

- Don't swim or surf between dusk and dawn – sharks do most of their hunting by night, and they're more likely to mistake you for prey in the dim light.
- Avoid swimming in murky or polluted waters for the same reason.
- Don't wear shiny jewellery – it looks like fish scales when the light reflects off it.
- Don't swim with open wounds or cuts – sharks are attracted by blood.
- Stay close to the shallows, where sharks are less likely to venture.
- And above all, avoid wearing an all-in-one turtle costume. It really won't help.

Fear Facts:

- Sharks have been around for over 400 million years – since long before the dinosaurs even existed.

- Great White Sharks are actually very intelligent, and have their own personalities and emotions.*
- Sharks never run out of teeth – when they lose one, it's quickly replaced by another growing in a 'backup row' just behind. An average shark may go through over 20,000 teeth during its life.

---

* Which means, out there somewhere, there's probably a Shy Shark, an Emo Shark, and an Evil Genius Shark. I'm not sure if that makes them more scary or less scary . . .

The hunter becomes the hunted

'Doug could tell it was coming fast, but he couldn't see it. Suddenly, the leopard exploded out of the bush only ten feet in front of them, leaping for Doug. Doug tried to raise his rifle but the speed of the cat was too great. He shot underneath the leopard as it hit him and knocked him backward. In its fury, the leopard bit down repeatedly on Doug's right hand and wrist, ripping through tendons and crippling his arm. At the same time, its back legs pumped up and down in a blur, raking Doug's belly in an attempt to disembowel him with its bladelike claws...'

From *Leopard Attack!* by John B. Snow

The fear

Lions, tigers and leopards could be thought of as the sharks of the land. They're clever, effective killers. They're deadly predators at the very top of their local food chain. And like sharks, they're very capable of attacking, maiming and devouring full-grown humans.

Big cats are lightning-fast and super-stealthy, so few people attacked by one ever see it coming. And once they pounce, there's little hope of escape. Leopards can run at 40mph, leap 6m horizontally and 3m vertically, and are excellent swimmers. The sheer size and power of a big cat will strike terror into anyone who sees one up close. Adult male lions reach lengths of over 2.5m

and weigh over 225kg. Siberian tigers have been known to reach 3.6m in length and over 363kg – over four times the weight of an average human male.

Oh yeah, and if you're pounced upon, you can more or less forget about trying to fight back. With one rake of razor-sharp claws or one bone-crushing bite to the neck, it's curtains for you and teatime for Tiddles. It's no wonder that some people fear these fearsome felines so much that even being stalked by a house cat will give them the heebie-jeebies.

The reality

There's no denying that lions, tigers and leopards can and do kill people. Nor are man-eating cats a problem of the past. Wild tigers alone kill between 40 and 60 people a year worldwide. In June 2004 Indian policemen captured three leopards that had killed more than 12 people in that month alone. And in September 2005 a pride of lions living near the Ethiopian capital of Addis Ababa killed at least 20 people (and over 750 livestock animals), causing over 1,000 people to flee their homes in terror. Even in the USA, where there are no wild tigers,* at least 14 people have been killed by tigers in zoos and private homes in the last decade.

But terrifying as these numbers sound, they don't really paint a fair picture of big-cat behaviour at all. As a matter of fact, big-cat attacks on people are extremely rare, and what we think of as 'man-eating' lions, tigers and leopards are rarer still.

Like most other predators, big cats attack for only two reasons – for food, or in self-defence. Left to themselves, few will attempt to hunt and eat a person. This is partly because we humans live in packs in clustered houses and settlements, making the preferred cat tactic of 'stalk and hunt' very difficult. Some of us also carry spears, guns and other things hazardous to a stalking cat. So, for the most part, the world's big cats have figured out that hunting humans is just not worth the trouble.

That said, if they're surprised, attacked, or protecting their young, most big cats will fight back ferociously. (You can hardly blame them for that – after all, we would probably do the same ourselves in such situations.) Otherwise, if a

---

* There are, of course, wild pumas (also known as *mountain lions* or *cougars*) in North America. But they almost never attack people unless provoked, so we won't bother worrying about them here. Likewise, jaguars (bigger and more powerful than leopards) roam the rainforests of South America. But jaguars aren't known to actually *hunt* people either. So we'll give those fearsome kitties a miss too.

lion, tiger or leopard spots a person, they'll generally either ignore them or move away, making it quite difficult to actually get close to them even if you want to.

So how do all those big-cat attacks we've already heard about happen? Well, the majority of attacks happen when people intrude on their wild territory, or when the cats are kept cooped-up in captivity – in zoos, circuses and even people's homes – and the keepers are foolish enough to try to play with them* or feed them by hand.

There are exceptions to this, of course. Sometimes, big cats do become people-killers. But this is usually because something has happened to make them become so. Tigers – the most common and successful maneaters – only usually begin to hunt people if their regular supply of prey (like deer and pigs) has been reduced by human hunters. Or it may sometimes begin when the tiger becomes old, sick or injured. In all these cases, the tiger is driven to hunt people out of desperation. There's no other way it can feed itself than to take what it can get, even if that means the risky tactic of hunting people.

Very occasionally, lions, tigers and leopards can become unusually unafraid of people and start to hunt them on purpose, *preferring* them to other prey. But these rogue

---

* Ever played with an over-excited house cat, and come away with scratches and bites for your trouble? Now imagine if that moggy was twice your height, four times your weight, and had two furry handfuls of razor-sharp knives rather than needle-like claws. If you still want to play with it *now*, then I wish you luck. Oh, and do you mind if I 'look after' your DVD collection while you're gone?

'killer cats' are the rarest type of all, and they're most often hunted down before they can do too much damage. It's fair to say that humans don't make up a regular part of the big-cat diet, and the average person has far more chance of dying after falling out of bed than they do of becoming lunch for a lion, tiger or leopard.*

The chances

If you don't live in India, Africa, south-east Asia or any other place where big cats still run wild, you're basically talking about getting mauled or killed by an escaped or captive animal. By far the most captive cats are kept in the USA, where there are actually five or six times as many tigers kept as pets than there are left in the wild worldwide. Even there, only one person a year is killed by a big cat – almost always a zookeeper or a misguided pet-tiger owner, rather than a random, unlucky person on the street. So outside of the Asian jungles and African plains, your odds of death-by-big-kitty are less than 1 in 3,000,000.

If you do live in wild big-cat territory, then your chances are, of course, quite a bit higher. But even then, your odds are much better than they used to be. While tigers currently kill around 50 or more people a year in India (about half of them in the Sundarban forest region, on the border between India and Bangladesh), around a century ago over *1,000 people per year* were being killed. Unfortunately there are a

---

* And you'd have to be *really* unlucky to fall out of bed and *on to* a lion, tiger or leopard. Although this is another great argument for not keeping them as pets.

few places in Africa and India where lion, tiger and leopard attacks are increasing, partly as a result of overpopulation, deforestation and people settling within big-cat territories. But for the most part the number of big-cat attacks are dropping, along with the number of cats themselves.

The lowdown

As a rule, big cats don't usually seek to attack people, and would much rather avoid human contact given the choice. When they're *not* given the choice, they do, occasionally, become dangerous maneaters. But these cases are very rare, and even if you're out on safari in Africa or India, you're extremely unlikely to be attacked, since they only really hunt people whom they find alone and helpless, rather than whole groups of people in jeeps.

If you are on a trip like this, then you can stay safe by simply staying in your vehicle. Every year at least one idiot tourist has a close encounter with a lion because he or she decides to get out and take a photograph.*

Lions, tigers and leopards, being cats, are also very curious. So if you're camping out in big-cat territory, it's not a good idea to leave your tent or hut door open at night – unless you want to wake up nose-to-whisker with a surprised carnivore four times your size.

Take these precautions, and there's little to fear from big cats, even in big-cat territory.

---

* Use a zoom lens, genius – it's much easier and much safer.

In fact we humans are far more of a danger to big cats than they are to us. Fewer than 3 in 1,000 tigers become maneaters, yet the total number of tigers left in the wild worldwide is less than 7,000. This is mostly due to hunting and habitat destruction by humans. The South China Tiger, the Amur Leopard and the Asiatic Lion are all either critically endangered or on the verge of extinction.

So if anyone should be afraid, it's not *us*, it's *them*.

MY 'KILLER CAT' EXPERIENCE

When I was about five years old, my family lived in a house in Kent with a huge back garden full of apple trees and gooseberry bushes. I'd often sneak down to the gooseberry bush and pick the sour green berries before they were ripe, and give myself a stomach ache eating big handfuls of them.

One day, I was deep in the gooseberry bush picking berries when a cat leaped on to my head from above. It was a neighbourhood tom cat – big, but certainly no tiger or leopard – and it had apparently mistaken my mop of hair for a bird. (Either that, or it was psychotic. I never did find out which.) The cat pounced and landed on my head with all four paws, piercing my scalp with its sharp claws and hanging on as I jumped up and cried out in panic for my dad.

My dad was in the garden too, building a new wall for the patio. So there he is, happily laying bricks, when all of a sudden his five-year-old son runs screaming towards him, his face streaming with blood and a furry cat-shaped hat perched on his head.

The cat and my dad locked eyes. The cat seemed to realize its mistake, and made a run for it. My dad picked up a house brick and ran after it, hurdling garden fences in his bright blue socks and jeans as he ran. In anger, but not really meaning to hurt the cat, he threw the brick. It missed the cat by approximately 20 metres (and 90 degrees) and instead smashed into a glass aviary in which one of our elderly neighbours kept his collection of pet birds. The birds flew everywhere. The old man shouted, 'Oi!' My dad offered a breathless apology. The killer cat was long gone.

A few days later an old lady who lived at the end of the street came to the house with a box of chocolates. The killer cat was hers. By now, all the neighbours had heard about the killer cat attack and the crazy birdhouse-destroying, fence-hurdling bricklayer, so she had come to apologize for her cat's behaviour. 'He's never done anything like that before,' she said.

We all felt guilty that this poor little old lady should feel so bad. After all, it wasn't her fault, and it wasn't really the cat's fault, either. He just thought he'd nabbed the biggest bird in cat history. Still, I didn't feel guilty enough to refuse the apology. Or the chocolates.'

Playing dead doesn't work

Bears, it's said, are almost dog-like in their behaviour. They're curious and intelligent, yet moody and unpredictable. In Canada and the USA, there are countless stories of bears attacking hikers and hunters, yet few can offer any helpful advice of what to do if you encounter one. Some say 'climb a tree', yet most bears are very good climbers. Some say 'run', yet a bear can hit speeds of 30–35 mph at a full charge. Others say 'curl up and play dead', yet at least one bear-attack victim tried this, and found herself bitten through the shoulder and shaken like a dog's toy. In the powerful jaws of the world's largest and smartest carnivores, sadly playing dead just doesn't work.

The fear

The fear of dogs is called *cynophobia*, and it's far more common than the fear of their larger, more ferocious cousins: wolves, hyenas and bears. But in all these cases, it's pretty much the same thing people are afraid of. It's not the bark or the howl . . . it's the *bite*.

ACK! ACK! ACK!

Picture this: a snarling, drooling muzzle wraps around your leg, and terrible yellow fangs tear lumps of flesh from your bones. Then it snaps again at your arms, your throat or your face.

Not scary enough for ya? Then try these little snippets for size.

Fear Facts:

- Enraged grizzly bears can charge, attack and kill even after being shot three or four times (the bullets often do little to stop them – they just seem to make the bear angrier).

- Hyenas have jaws so powerful that they can crush bones in a single bite, and they've been known to attack African villagers asleep on the ground outside their huts, biting their faces right off.

Wolves attack in pairs or packs, tearing their victims to shreds. And many of their tamer relatives are quite capable of doing the very same thing. Although we've come to love dogs as companions and guardians, pet dogs bite literally *millions* of people every year. Which kind of makes you wonder if that whole 'man's best friend' thing is right after all . . .

The reality

Fearsome as they are, bears – like most wild animals – very rarely attack people unless they're startled, cornered, provoked, or defending their young. So, for the most part, all you have to do to avoid a bear attack is make sure not to do any of those things when hiking through bear country. And since bears usually try their hardest to avoid people anyway, this is generally quite easy to do.

Although they have fairly poor eyesight, bears have excellent hearing and a keen sense of smell. So they will usually amble away before you can get within a kilometre of them. This makes your chances of spotting one – let alone wrestling one – pretty slim in the first place. Even if you are lucky (or rather, unlucky) enough to stumble upon one, most will just growl or pretend to charge at you in an effort to get you to back off and leave them alone. If you do the right things when this happens, you should be able to do just that – retreat and escape unharmed.

As for wolves and hyenas, they're mostly scavenging hunters that take advantage of the weak. They very rarely attack healthy, moving humans, as we seem too strong and too much trouble. Despite the wolf's 'big, bad' reputation, there are hardly any reports of hyena or wolf packs attacking and eating living people.*

Domestic dogs, however, are another story. Experts reckon that around 8% of all dogs will bite somebody during the course of their lives. How dangerous they are depends on the breed, where they are when you encounter them and – perhaps most of all – how they've been trained and treated. Some dogs are pretty much harmless. Others are very loving with their owners, but nasty and aggressive with everyone else. Still others are a danger to anyone they encounter. The trick is in telling the difference, and not doing things that provoke dogs into attacking.

All dogs are territorial animals, and most dog attacks happen in the owner's home or garden rather than out and about. Dogs kept chained up are also more likely to bite than those on leads or running free. This shows that most attacks

---

* Although, being efficient scavengers, many wouldn't think twice about scoffing you if they found you lying dead or unconscious somewhere. This is what happens when hyenas bite people sleeping outdoors in Africa. 'Hey,' they think, 'maybe this guy isn't *using* his face any more. Waste not, want not . . .'

happen when the dog feels trapped, cornered or defensive of its own turf.

Toddlers under four are the most common age group for dog-attack victims. This is partly because they tend to approach dogs with flailing limbs and sudden motions (often pulling and grabbing at the ears, tail or fur of the 'nice goggie' as they investigate it). And although dogs of any breed can bite or attack if provoked, most of the fatal attacks come from some of those dog breeds that are bred specifically to be ferocious fighters or guard dogs, such as Pit Bulls, Rottweilers and German Shepherds.

The chances

While minor dog bites are fairly common worldwide, serious dog attacks are far less common, and deaths from dog attacks are very rare. In the USA, for example, there are roughly 4.7 million dog attacks per year, meaning that about 1.5% of the population will be bitten by a dog during a single year.* But only around 6,000 (0.1%) of these attacks require a trip to the hospital, and only 30 or so (or 0.000006%) result in death – usually of a toddler or an elderly person. Overall, your chances of being attacked and killed by a dog are less than 1 in 150,000.

Grizzly bears and brown bears kill an average of two unlucky people per year, while the less aggressive black

---

* Not that the USA has particularly dangerous dogs – it's just where the best records and figures for dog attacks are kept. Largely so that people can sue dog owners when they're bitten.

bears score just one. As for deaths related to wolves and hyenas, the annual average is almost zero. Because of this, weighing up the odds of being attacked and killed by a bear, a wolf or a hyena is difficult, but it's probably many millions to one.

The lowdown

Very few of us will ever come across a wolf or hyena outside of a zoo, and since attacks from them on people are so rare anyway, we can pretty much stop worrying about them straight away.

Bears, however, are quite widespread in parts of northern Europe, North America and northern Asia. Even so, the chances of being attacked and killed by a bear are still very small, and if you treat bears with caution and respect, your chances become even smaller. This includes doing the following:

- As a rule, avoid encountering a bear wherever possible. (This might sound obvious, but many a hiker has been attacked because they spotted a cuddly-looking bear in the forest, then went in for a closer look rather than retreating.)
- Make plenty of noise as you walk through regions known to contain bears, so that they can hear you coming and move away. Singing is good for this, provided it's not a Britney Spears song. This won't annoy the bear, but it may annoy your friends.

If you do accidentally find a bear (or a bear finds you), then identify yourself as human by talking loudly and waving your arms. If the bear charges, don't run – most charges are 'fake outs' that stop short of hitting you, and the bear will often move off once he's made his point. (Besides, you'll never outrun a bear anyway, and running might even encourage him to chase you.)

If that doesn't work, you have two choices: play dead, or fight back. Playing dead can work if the bear is being defensive, but if it's looking at you as food, your best chance is to fight. And your best weapon is – believe it or not – a can of chilli-pepper spray. A bear spray can fire a cloud of stinging gas over 8m, targeting the bear's sensitive nose. In tests, it has been found close to 100% effective, and is a far better option than guns or kung-fu . . .

As for dogs, well, they're everywhere. But again, dog attacks (especially fatal ones) are extremely rare, and a few sensible measures will help you avoid becoming a victim of the few 'bad apples' in the doggie barrel.

Don't approach and attempt to pet a strange dog unless *invited* to by the owner, and *even if* you are invited, always allow the dog to approach and sniff you first before shooting out a hand to scratch and pat it.

If you're in a dog's (or rather a dog-owner's) home or garden for the first time, be especially wary of approaching the dog before you're sure the dog is at ease. (It should go without saying that climbing into a strange dog's kennel while making cat noises is a big no-no.)

Look for warning signs, like low growls or the dog purposely holding its head level with the body (as opposed to lower or higher) – this can signal an angry dog, so it's best to leave it well alone.

If the worst happens, and you feel you are about to be attacked, there are still things you can do. Stay calm, don't run, and turn side-on to the dog, while avoiding eye contact. In dog language, this tells the dog you're not threatening it, while also not submitting to it. Usually the dog will lose interest after a bit of barking and posturing, and you can back slowly away from it.

Do all this, and your chances of being attacked – which are already very small – are much lower, and you can start to enjoy being around dogs rather than afraid of them. For the most part, dogs are loyal, friendly companions. Treat them carefully and kindly, and there's little to fear from them.

Fangs for the memory

'Like still-frame images, I remember looking at my hand after feeling an unusual and slightly painful sensation. The sight of two holes oozing blood and urine-coloured venom sent my heart well into my throat . . . I could already feel a numbing in my lips, head and arms, and each step I took got clumsier and clumsier . . . Swallowing became a challenge. My vision distorted, making the world look as if I were viewing it from behind a dusty windshield.'

From *I Should Be Dead* by Peter Jenkins

The fear

OK, in the Top 10 Terrifying Animals list, we've now reached the two chart-toppers. The fear of spiders (*arachnophobia*) and the fear of snakes (*ophidiophobia*) are easily the most common animal-related fears. The fear of snakes, in particular, seems to be shared across all the cultures and peoples of the world. Even in places like the Arctic, where there are no snakes at all and no one has even *seen* a snake before, the native people are still wary of snakes when first introduced to them by others.

And why not? I mean, when one bite could lead to terrible pain (not to mention swollen and paralysed muscles, internal bleeding, blood clots, kidney failure, heart attack . . .), doesn't it make sense to run screaming from every snake or spider you see?

The reality

Well . . . not really. Most snakes and spiders aren't venomous at all, and even the venomous ones aren't as dangerous as they seem. For the most part, anyway.

Of the 2,500 to 3,000 species of snake on the planet, only around six or seven hundred (20–25%) are actually venomous, and only a third of those (including Cobras, Rattlesnakes, Adders, Kraits, Vipers, Brown snakes and Taipans) are capable of killing with a single bite.

'Oh *great*,' I hear you say. '*Only* 25 per cent? That's just *wonderful.*' But if you think about it, this means over three-quarters of the snakes in the world pose *no threat to people* whatsoever.

What's more, just because a snake is venomous, that doesn't mean it likes to bite people. Most snakes – venomous snakes included – will try to avoid biting people where they can, and, if possible, avoid interacting with people altogether. Snakes are actually very shy creatures, and the vast majority of bites happen to people who try to catch, handle or kill them. Even when cornered or threatened, many 'deadly' snakes will give you easy-to-spot warnings before striking out – signs like rearing up, flattening their heads, and hissing and 'feinting' with pretend strikes to scare you off. Spot these signs and step out of range (most snakes can only strike within a distance equal to half the length of their bodies), and you're safe.[*]

Fear Facts:

- While most snakes have teeth, only venomous snakes have fangs. Some snakes have hinged fangs which fold back and up against the roof of the mouth, but swing forward and down just before they bite.
- All snakes are carnivores and swallow their food whole. Snakes eat everything from insects, rodents and birds to turtles, pigs and small deer.

---

[*] This is not, however, an encouragement to try and guess how long a dangerous snake is, and then dance around it in a circle roughly half that snake-length away) chanting 'C'mon then, snakey! Gimme yer best shot!' Humans are notoriously bad at judging lengths and distances correctly by eye. And no self-respecting cobra will let you get near it with a tape measure – so don't try that either.

- The smallest snake in the world was recently discovered on the Caribbean island of Barbados, and measures just 100mm (less than 4 inches) in length. It has been nicknamed the *microsnake*.
- The largest snake in the world is the Asian reticulated python, which reaches up to 15m in length. The South American Giant Anaconda is a bit shorter, at around 9m, but is much thicker and heavier, with some weighing over 200kg!

As for spiders, there are over 40,000 known species, yet fewer than 30 have venom that can cause serious illness in humans, and only a few (including Black and Brown Widow spiders, Funnel Web spiders and Brazilian Wandering spiders) are capable of killing with a bite. This is because spider venom typically only works on the animals (usually insects, but sometimes birds and small mammals) that the spider preys on. So most venomous spider bites cause, at worst, minor illness in humans and other animals not part of the spider's diet.

In fact, most of the spiders people think are 'deadly' aren't even that dangerous. A bite from a Tarantula, for example, is very painful but certainly won't kill you. A bite from the Brown Recluse spider may look nasty, as it causes the flesh around it to rot and die, but there hasn't been a single confirmed death from one of those either.

Even Black Widows, which do have the ability to kill us, hardly ever succeed in doing so, because they rarely inject more than a tiny amount of venom per bite. Add to that the powerful antivenins (medicines which work against the venom of specific spiders and snakes) that are kept in hospitals to treat Black Widow bites, and the result is that the death rate has fallen to just one or two people per year, worldwide.

And just like snakes, most spiders are not aggressive, and prefer not to get close enough to humans to bite them. In fact, most spiders are even less keen on biting than snakes, and only bite if picked up, prodded or squashed. No venomous spider will charge or jump at you to bite, like they do in horror movies. Almost all spider bites happen when people put on gloves, footwear or other clothing in which the spider was resting. And think about it – if you were stuck in the toe of a giant boot, and a huge fleshy foot came down to squash you, what would you do? Everything you could to stop it, I should think. And that's all poor Spidey does.

The chances

So what are your chances of being killed by a deadly slitherer or scuttler?

Well, despite the unwillingness of most snakes to bite people, between 3 and 6 million people manage to get bitten by snakes every year, with over 90% of these bites typically happening in central Africa, India and south-east Asia.

But still, only 0.01 to 0.02% (1 or 2 in every 10,000 bites) result in death. So even if you are bitten, the average odds of surviving are over 99.98%!

For spiders, the number is a bit trickier to work out, as the vast majority of spider bites are never treated in hospitals or reported to spider researchers. But look at it this way – no spider species in the world is known to have a bite which kills over 10% of its victims. In Australia, where perhaps the most species of venomous spiders live, there have been no recorded deaths from spider bites (of any kind) since 1979. Brazilian Wandering spiders,* which are thought to have the most powerful venom of any spider in the world, have caused only a handful of deaths in over 7,000 recorded bites. So these days, spiders – even the 'deadly' ones – really aren't a major threat to us humans at all.

The lowdown

Spiders and snakes, basically, get a bad rap. Our fear of them is deep, because it goes way, way back – perhaps to the time when our primate ancestors used to sleep on forest floors or up in trees, where they encountered spiders and snakes more often.

At least part of our fear of them seems to be inborn. We know this because when monkeys, apes and human toddlers are shown snake-like shapes, they spot them

---

* This spider gets its name from the fact that it leaves its web to wander the forest floor in search of prey. Not because it gets lost a lot and scuttles about looking confused, perhaps holding a tiny map between two of its eight legs.

and react to them very quickly, even against a background of other similar objects. This suggests that humans (and some other animals) are *naturally* wary of snakes and spiders.

This is possibly because that very fear helped their ancestors to survive. While snake and spider bites rarely kill modern humans, it would have been a different story for our animal ancestors. One painful, swollen bite to the hand or foot could have stopped them from hunting.

That would have made even non-lethal snake and spider bites deadly in the long run. So nature would have filtered out those among our ancestors who were too curious, too unafraid and too easily bitten, leaving only the successful snake-and-spider-phobes behind.

But when you look at it, we really don't need these fears any more. Very few snakes (and hardly any spiders) pose a threat to us now, and they're generally easy enough to avoid, since we no longer have to go rooting around in the jungles and forests where most of the venomous ones live. If we don't meddle with snakes, then they'll generally leave us alone. And if we can tolerate having spiders around, they actually do us a favour by removing mosquitoes, flies and other bothersome insects as part of their daily diet.

If you do come across a strange spider or snake, and you're unsure if it's dangerous or not, then dealing with it is simple. Just leave it alone, or, if it's in your house, call a vet or professional animal handler to come and remove it for you. Remember, very few people get bitten by snakes or spiders at all, but most of the ones that *do* get bitten were trying to catch, handle or kill them at the time. Snakes and spiders very rarely strike . . . unless they're *striking back*.

If snakes or spiders genuinely give you the creeps, you may never be happy having them in your house or feeding them crickets while you curl up on the sofa. But that doesn't mean you can't share the planet with them. Even life of the slithering and scuttling variety deserves our respect and protection.

So no more washing that spider down the plughole, please. Just trap him in a cup and lob him outside instead. There. Doesn't that feel better?

Fear Facts:

All spiders have a pair of hollow fangs, which they use to inject venom into prey, but most are unable to pierce human skin with their bite.

All spiders are carnivorous (meat-eaters) and they prey mostly on insects like flies, moths, mosquitoes and ants. But some prey instead on frogs, lizards, snakes, birds and other spiders.

There are two basic kinds of spider venom – neurotoxic and necrotic. Neurotoxic venoms affect the nerves throughout the body, causing muscle cramps, paralysis and (very occasionally) death. Necrotic toxins destroy skin and muscle cells, causing blistering and blackening of the area around the bite. Snake venom can contain a combination of both of these types, and may also contain haemolytic toxins (which destroy your blood cells) and anticoagulants (which stop your blood from clotting).

The smallest spider in the world is the Samoan Web-building Spider, *Patu marplesi*, which measures just 0.43mm across. The largest is the South American Goliath Birdeater (a type of tarantula), which can be up to 30cm across.

Bee afraid, bee very afraid

The Asian Giant Hornet (*Vespa mandarinia*) is, technically, the world's largest wasp. At 5cm long, and with a wingspan as wide as your palm, it looks more like a small bird than an insect. Until, that is, you spot the yellow-and-black-striped colouring, or the 6mm-long sting. Being stung by one feels like having a small nail driven into you, as the potent venom it injects begins to eat away at the membranes of your skin. What's more, it can fly at up to 25mph, and it regularly attacks humans.

The fear

Bugs. Creepy-crawlies. Ugh! Scuttling, biting, stinging insects have a special place in the world of animal fears. While not everyone is actually *afraid* of them, most of us are wary of at least one type of insect, and maybe more. And the thought of being covered in swarms of them only multiplies the imagined horrors in your head. Don't believe me? OK, try this one for size . . .

Picture in your mind, as clearly as you can, playing outside in a park on a warm summer's day. A friend kicks a football towards you, but it misses, strikes a papery nest in a tree just behind you, and within seconds your head is surrounded by a thick cloud of angry, buzzing wasps, jabbing you over and over with their vicious, painful stings.

Or how about this: out camping near the edge of a wide, rocky desert, you slip your bare legs into your sleeping bag, and suddenly find it filled with scuttling cockroaches ... or centipedes ... or scorpions ...

Yep. Creepy-crawlies got their name for a reason. They give most people the creeps.

The reality

As with snakes and spiders, most insects aren't much of a threat to us at all, and yet we freak out at the sight of them through a combination of instinctive and learned reactions. Because they scuttle and buzz so quickly, their quick, erratic movements can sometimes set off our startle reflexes, making our heart rate rise and breathing quicken. But that just means we've *noticed* them, and if we didn't hear all sorts of horror stories about bug bites and bee stings, then most of us wouldn't be *anywhere near* as wary of insects as we are. After all, for the most part insects are very helpful to us, and practically none of them are actually what we'd call 'dangerous'.

For starters, unless you're allergic to them, no bee, wasp or hornet on the planet can kill a human with a single sting. The average honey bee would have to sting you over 10,000 times to even get close, and since each bee dies after one sting, that's not likely to happen unless you bellyflop on to a hive and roll around on it.*

What about killer scorpions? Well, again – not really. Like their spider cousins (spiders and scorpions fall into the same class of animals, called *Arachnids*), the venoms of most scorpions only affect the bodies of the insects they prey on. Plus, they usually paralyse rather than kill. In humans, scorpion stings usually cause little more than a bit of swelling and numbness. Even those, like the Deathstalker,** that are capable of killing people rarely inject enough venom to actually kill a healthy adult human. In fact, almost all scorpion victims are either very young, very old or very sick. As for the other venomous insects – like fire ants, blister beetles and a few types of hairy caterpillar – some of them could certainly make you ill, but none of them could actually 'do you in' with their bite or sting.

---

* Not clever. Don't try. Full stop.

** Which is also, without doubt, the animal with the coolest, scariest name in the world. If a bunch of Deathstalker scorpions formed a rock band, they'd just use their own name. You can't top that.

The only real danger we face from insects (except m
ticks and mosquitoes – but more about that in a minu.
comes from being allergic to them. If you're allergic,
then harmless bites and stings can quickly turn into life-
threatening conditions. If you do have such an allergy, then
fearing bites and stings is understandable. But it's also
worth bearing in mind that most allergies are very specific
– so you might be allergic to bee stings, but not wasp or
hornet stings. Plus, with treatment at a hospital, even very
nasty allergic reactions can be controlled if they're handled
quickly.

The chances

Unless you're allergic to them, the odds of being killed
by a wasp, bee or hornet sting are around 1 in 6,000,000
– in other words: extremely, EXTREMELY unlikely. If
you are allergic, the odds are quite a bit higher, so you
really do need to be careful around them. (Each year,
allergic reactions to bee stings kill more people than
spider bites and snake bites put together.) As for ants,
beetles, scorpions and most other insects, your chances
of being seriously harmed by one of those are practically
zero.

The lowdown

Like it or not, insects are here to stay. There are between
10 million and 30 million species of them worldwide,
and five out of every six animals found on land is an

insect. They were here before us and they'll probably be here long after we're gone. So we're going to have to learn to live with them. The good news, as we've seen, is that very few insect species can do us any serious harm through bites and stings, and almost none of the insects we see creeping, crawling and buzzing around us are dangerous in any way. So hooray for the friendly bugs!

In fact, the only truly dangerous insects are ones we can hardly see, with bites we can hardly feel. Ticks and mosquitoes can be a real danger to human health – not because their bites are venomous, but because they carry with them dangerous microorganisms that can cause deadly diseases. Ticks can spread Lyme's disease and the brain disease encephalitis, while mosquitoes carry diseases that include malaria, dengue fever, yellow fever and many more.

Happily, you can actually avoid being bitten while in areas where ticks and mosquitoes live and breed. All you have to do is wear clothing that covers your arms, legs and head, use a good insect repellent, and check yourself for unwelcome hitchhikers when you return from a hike through swamps, fields or forests.*

As for bees and wasps, if you're allergic to stings, then

---

* I recently found a tick on the back of my neck after a short hike in a forest close to where I live. By the time I finally felt it and plucked it off, it had guzzled several times its own weight in fresh blood, and looked quite pleased with itself. In the end, I decided to throw it outside on the grass rather than kill it. Luckily for the tick, my motto – like my blood type – is 'B positive'.

you definitely want to avoid being stung (and even if you're not allergic, it's still a good idea, as it's never pleasant)! To do that:

- Don't wear perfumes or scented lotions if you're heading outside – they can attract confused bees and wasps like flower scents.
- Avoid picking flowers or walking barefoot in the garden when bees are busy with pollinating nearby.
- If you find a nest near the house, don't go near it. Call someone to relocate or dispose of it safely.
- Keep sweet fruits and soft drinks covered up, or leave them indoors. Strong sugary scents will bring wasps from miles around.

With a few exceptions, insects aren't just safe, they're overwhelmingly helpful* little creatures for us to have around. They help maintain our environment by gardening for us (pollinating flowers, eating plant pests and weeds), they dispose of animal droppings, they nourish the soil, and they provide us with honey, silk, dyes, medicines and more. Without them, our world wouldn't be a very nice place to live in. So start thinking about them that way, and let's all try to get along, shall we?

---

* Yep, even wasps. They not only pollinate flowers, but also kill pesky flies and crop pests. So they're not *all* bad!

THE HORDE OF HORRIBLE HORNETS

'When I was about thirteen, my parents, my brother and I drove from England to northern Italy, where my sister had been living and working for the previous two years. We stayed in a converted farmhouse surrounded by a vineyard – all yellow stone, thick wooden doors and beautiful trees, vines and flowers. One night, around dusk, my brother and I were sitting outside with our sketchbooks. Coming over all arty, we decided to sit and draw the flowers in a bush right outside our open front doorway. After about half an hour of sketching, what looked like two or three small birds arrived and started hovering around the flowers. They had fat yellow-and-black-striped bodies and eyes that seemed to glow in the dark.

'Look at those hummingbirds,' said my brother. 'Lovely, aren't they? You don't get those in England.'

'You don't get hummingbirds like *those* anywhere,' I replied. 'Those things are . . . big wasps or something'.

'Nahh,' said my brother, 'no wasp is that big . . . unless it's a hornet. But . . . nahhh, they're not *that* big either, are they?'

'I'm not sticking around to find out,' I replied,

and slowly rose from my chair, backing through the door and keeping both eyes on the hornets in case I had to run for it. Eventually I turned and legged it into the living room.

'Dad! Dad! There's hornets outside!' I yelped, 'Proper massive ones!'

'Nahhhhh,' said my dad, sounding exactly like my brother, 'you don't get hornets in Italy.'

He went to investigate anyway, taking his glass of beer with him. My brother, meanwhile, had decided that his 'hummingbirds' just might be hornets after all. There were more of them now – maybe ten or twenty. So he picked up his drink and backed slowly towards the door, as I had before him. Just as he was turning away from the hovering hornets, a vine growing across the door brushed his arm. He yelped, thinking that a stray hornet had attacked him, and in one twitchy reflex flung his drink down the hallway. My dad, seeing this, roared with laughter, calling my brother 'a big girl's blouse' and pushing past him to see the hornets he was so sure did not exist.

Then he saw them.

'Bloomin' 'ell!' he said, and quickly retreated towards the doorway. What happened next was pure comedy genius. Brushing against the same vine that had spooked my brother, he too yelped and threw his drink down the hallway. My brother and I laughed until tears streamed down our cheeks. Eventually my dad joined in.

The next day we told the owner of the farmhouse, and he called out somebody to find and remove the nest. 'If a couple of those stung you, you'd be in the hospital,' he said. He was probably right, but, to be fair, they hadn't *tried* to sting us, and I don't think they would have even if we had decided to stay put instead of running. So now when I think of hornets, I laugh rather than cringe.

2 Natural Disasters

Big + Unexpected = Scary

Why is it that some things seem so scary that just thinking about them can make you frightened? If you've never experienced an earthquake, never seen a tornado, and never been struck by lightning, why would a gentle tremor or a distant rumble of thunder make you jumpy? And why is it some people hardly seem to notice these things while others tremble and cry out?

The answer lies in your head. Or, more specifically, in your brain.

Fear, in a sense, comes in two parts, both of which are triggered and created inside your brain. The first part is the *emotion* of fear. The second part is the *feeling* of fear.

But hang on a minute – aren't emotions and feelings the same thing? Well . . . not quite.

An emotion is actually *a series of changes that occur in*

your body. These changes usually happen as it responds to something it has just sensed (seen, heard, smelt, touched or tasted). Happiness, for example, could be triggered by the sound of birds chirping outside your window or the taste of chocolate on your tongue. The most obvious change this causes in your body is smiling.

Surprise and disgust are emotions too. They might be triggered if, for example, you slip and fall over on the street. This might cause your eyes and mouth to snap open – physical changes that come with surprise. Then, as you see the squashed slug on your shoe, your mouth might narrow and turn down at the edges. This is a physical change linked to disgust.*

The emotion of fear, however, involves different physical signs – like sweaty palms, widened pupils, and a quickened heartbeat. As fear builds, it might make you tremble, freeze, faint, or even lose control of your bladder or bum muscles. How far it goes depends partly on how big the trigger (or stimulus) is that starts it off. So just as *eating* a slug might trigger more disgust than slipping on one, a deafening crack of thunder will trigger more fear than a gently popping balloon. But it also depends on how *unexpected* the stimulus is. That's why popping a balloon yourself is far less likely to scare you than having someone sneak up and pop one right behind your head.

---

* Interestingly, most people tend to say 'uuuuuuuuuuurrghh!' in this kind of situation too – a word which seems to mean 'That's surprisingly revolting!' in almost all known languages.

Does that all sound a bit obvious? Well, if it does, then hold on – because that's only half the story.

Aside from the emotion of fear, there's also the *feeling* of fear. While an emotion is a series of changes that occurs in your body, a feeling is *how you experience and explain those bodily changes* in your brain. The feeling of fear is actually created in a different part of the brain to the emotion of fear (the emotion in the centre, the feeling kind of around the outer edges and towards the front), and this is part of the reason why different people respond differently to the same 'scare triggers' or stimuli.[*]

When it comes to being big and unexpected, you don't get much bigger or more startling than natural disasters, like storms, tornadoes and earthquakes. So for all of us, these are pretty big triggers for the emotion of fear. But just because they're big, powerful and (let's face it) dangerous, that doesn't mean we need to live in fear of them. For starters, the chances of getting hit by a lightning bolt or tornado are pretty small in most parts of the world. And even where huge storms and tornadoes are more common, there are often simple ways to avoid them, making living with them much safer.

The difference between being terrified and being unafraid is often just a matter of *how much you know*

---

[*] *Stimuli*, by the way, is the plural word for stimulus, just as *fungi* (rather than *funguses*) correctly describes a bunch of mushrooms. Confusingly, the plurals of *octopus* and *platypus* are not *octopi* and *platypi*, but *octopuses* and *platypuses*. You can blame the Greeks for this. I always do, anyway.

and *how prepared you are*. If you know how storms and earthquakes work, and you know how to deal with them, then you can change how you feel about them and cope much better with the emotions of fear they create. You can actually use the logical, thinking part of your brain to partly override the emotional part.

Everybody experiences the emotion of fear, but how we *feel* fear is up to us.

A very dodgy line

'No one ever told me you weren't supposed to be on a land-line telephone during an electrical storm. So, there I was, calling in a carryout pizza order, when I noticed that the lightning and thunder was getting more intense, and coming more frequently. Then I heard static on the phone line, which kept getting louder and louder. Then I heard what sounded like a loud explosion, and at the same time I noticed a bright, white light at my feet, which was football-shaped, and had spikes. It blew me across the floor, and I was knocked out for a few seconds.

My son came running into the kitchen, to find me laying there on the floor.'

Lightning survivor 'Missy', USA

The fear

Astraphobia, or the fear of thunder and lightning, is one of the most common fears in the world. And for good reason – lightning is truly terrifying stuff. At over 30,000 °C, a bolt of lightning is five to six times hotter than the surface of the Sun. Each bolt moves so fast that not even a ninja could dodge it. A single lightning strike contains over a billion volts of electricity at a current of up to 160,000 amperes. That's enough to power a light bulb for over three months, and 2–3 million times more powerful than it needs to be in order to kill you.

Lightning doesn't play fair either. It can rip through buildings and vehicles, and it can hit whole crowds of people at once. If the main strike misses you and hits something else, it can 'splash' from nearby objects and zap you anyway, or travel through the ground and hit you from the feet up. Even if it misses you entirely, the shockwave caused by the exploding air around it can knock you flat, break your ribs and burst your eardrums. And what if it struck while you were flying in an aeroplane? Would the plane explode or fall out of the sky? If it hit your speeding car, would you be blown off the road? And if it can even hit you *indoors* down the telephone line, then surely there's no escape! Gaaaaaaagh!

The reality

OK, so there's no getting around it – lightning is definitely very dangerous stuff. Triggered by a build-up of charged particles within massive clouds, a bolt of lightning literally rips the air apart as it goes, travelling at over 136,000 mph and reaching temperatures hot enough to melt iron. No one wants to mess with that.

That's part of the reason why we (like most other animals) have evolved to be jumpy at the boom and flash of thunder and lightning. It's a pretty healthy fear to have, and one that has kept us and our animal ancestors alive for thousands of years. The huge noise, temperature and electric current that come with lightning can trigger a very strong fear response. But knowing a little more about how lightning works can help us keep our reactions to lightning under control.

There are several types of lightning, including cloud-to-ground (CG), cloud-to-cloud (CC), in-cloud (IC), cloud-to-air (CA) and ball lightning. But all of these only happen within (or around) a certain type of cloud – the thundercloud, called *cumulonimbus*. The cumulonimbus is a huge, dark, towering monster of a cloud, so it's pretty easy to spot and avoid. And simple as it sounds, that's pretty much all there is to it: avoid being out in a thunderstorm, and you have very little to fear from lightning.

This is because lightning, or at least the cloud-to-ground type that poses a threat to us, only really wants to do one thing – connect a thundercloud to the ground (through the air) so that it can release its built-up electric charge. But since air doesn't conduct electricity too well, lightning usually (but not always) strikes the tallest thing around in an effort to avoid travelling through too much air. That's why it often hits tall towers, buildings and trees – the towering wood, metal and concrete structures give the electric charge an easy path to the ground. This is easier than if it had to travel through *more* air to flow through objects or people closer to the ground.

This is also why it's generally quite safe indoors during thunderstorms. If lightning does hit your building, then it already has a nice, easy path to the ground through the walls (especially if they contain handy metal pipes or electric cables), so why would it force its way through the air inside just to hit you and your mates? Of course, if you offer it a new path to you through a telephone cable or a gadget plugged into the mains, then you're asking for an indoor zapping . . .

The same goes for cars and aeroplanes, which are both – as a matter of fact – quite safe places to be when lightning strikes. The cage-like metal structure of cars usually channels the electric charge safely around the passengers inside, leaving them totally unharmed – although it may melt the tyres, knock out the electrical systems and stop the engine. Aeroplanes, in a sense, are even safer. They're specifically built to channel lightning strikes around the passengers and fuel tank, through the use of metal shielding in the outer skin and walls. In fact, lightning strikes airliners all the time, but the passengers rarely notice!

The chances

The odds of getting hit by lightning vary, depending on where you live, how many thunderstorms that area gets, and how much time you spend outside. So it can range from about 1 in 80,000 (highly unlikely) to 1 in 400,000 (almost never gonna happen). But your odds of being hit are hugely affected by how you behave during storms.

Lightning kills about 10,000 people a year worldwide – more people each year than tornadoes, flooding or any other kind of bad weather. But it's worth noting that almost all of these people were outside in a thunderstorm at the time, many of them working in fields, hiking, fishing, boating, playing golf or running about in open sports grounds. Remove these 'extreme farmers and sports fans' from the figures, and fewer than a couple of hundred remain (which in a world of over 6 billion people ain't too bad). Less than 1% of lightning victims are hit indoors, and most of those are on the telephone at the time (a good reason to stay off the phone during storms too).

The lowdown

So in short, lightning *is* scary stuff, but you needn't be afraid of it as long as you stay smart and stay safe. In fact, as long as you respect it and take a few precautions, you're pretty much in the clear. Knowing that (and perhaps telling yourself that, as the storm rumbles and flashes on) is the first step towards changing how you *feel* about thunder and lightning. You may still get tense and short of breath (signs of the emotion of fear) when the thunder first cracks, but knowing how lightning works and behaves can help you control the feelings that follow, so that the fear gradually ebbs away.

Of course, knowing what to do during a storm will make you feel even better. And for the most part, that means calmly seeking shelter at the first rumblings of a thunderstorm. Don't wait for the rain, as lightning can sometimes strike ahead of the downpour. If you like, you can count the time between each thunderclap and lightning flash to work out how far off it is – just divide the number of seconds by 6, and you get the rough distance away (in miles) of the centre of the storm (so 30 seconds = 5 miles). But do this indoors. Then stay indoors until the storm has passed. Many lightning strikes actually happen at the edges of the cloud, making the beginning and end of a storm the most dangerous bits. You think, 'It's not here yet,' or, 'It's gone' . . . then BOOM!

If you're outside fishing, boating or playing sports, stop and go inside. Remember, being 'macho' or 'extreme' about lightning is the best way to end up as one of those 10,000 actual annual lightning victims. Finally, realize that 'take shelter' doesn't mean 'stand under a tree'. Quite the opposite, in fact. While the tree will shelter you from the rain, it may attract a lightning strike, and you're likely to be hit along with it.

If you really can't get in out of the storm, conventional wisdom has it that you should crouch down in a ball and hug your knees. That way, you make yourself as small a target as possible, and if the lightning does strike you, it should flow quickly from your head/neck to the ground – hopefully avoiding causing serious burns and nerve damage on the way through. But this really is a last resort, and shouldn't be relied upon. Even taking these precautions, if you are struck, you're just as likely to end up looking like a charred pebble as you are to escape unscathed.

One last happy fact to think about: believe it or not, lightning victims usually don't die. About 70–95% of the time they survive, often with just a few burns and scrapes.

Still – wouldn't want to try it, eh?

Fear Fact:

Jet airliners are struck by lightning, on average, at least once a year, every year. So a single jumbo jet may be hit 30 times or more during its normal lifespan of 100,000 takeoffs and landings!

Hit by a twister

'The roar of the storm grew louder. Windowpanes were cracking. Wind was blowing throughout the living room. Dishes, pots and paper were flying from the kitchen. Plaster was crumbling away from the walls. My mother Zena, my brother Gordon, and myself were on the first floor of the farmhouse when the tornado hit us. The roar was like a freight train. As the walls collapsed around us, knocking us down, we happened to fall beside the dining-room table. It was an old wooden farm table and it made a tiny space and barely held the walls from crushing us. My brother Tom was upstairs in his bedroom. He pulled the covers over his head. As the house collapsed, Tom's bed flew, and he wound up in the front yard.'

Survivor of the 1953 Beecher Tornado, USA

The fear

Few people like the idea of being engulfed by roaring, deafening winds and tossed around like a rag doll. Fewer still fancy being buried alive in sand, snow or bits of their own house. Desert sandstorms can blind or suffocate people. Violent snowstorms, called blizzards, can freeze you to death with their icy winds and leave you buried beneath metres of snow. And perhaps most frightening of all is the terrifying, concentrated power of the tornado, or 'twister'. Twisters can strip the bark off trees, turn cars into flying missiles, and flatten entire towns. You'd have to be daft not to be even a little bit alarmed by that.

The reality

Happily, sandstorms and blizzards aren't nearly as threatening as they seem – at least for most people on the planet. Formed by natural (but powerful) shifts of air between areas of high and low pressure, they're little more than strong winds carrying sand or frozen water.

Both tend not to happen outside the desert or snow-bound regions where people expect them to be. And even when they do surprise the locals, both types of storm are quite survivable. If you're caught outside in a sandstorm, a wet cloth over the nose and mouth will stop you choking on grains of flying sand, while proper cold-weather gear will insulate you and stop you from freezing to death in a blizzard. Prepared like this, you can usually seek shelter or higher ground before the sand or snow has a chance to bury and suffocate you. For the most part, sandstorms and snowstorms only pose a threat to travellers in remote areas, or to people cut off without food, water or power by drifting sand dunes and snow outside their houses. So if you live in the desert, high mountains or Arctic, you'd better be prepared. If you live elsewhere, don't sweat it – you're safe!

Tornadoes, on the other hand, are much more dangerous and far more frequent. Caught out in the open by a full-force twister, there's little to do but pray for a soft landing (and that's if you haven't already been peppered by bits of flying car and house). Some parts of the world – such as the famous 'Tornado Alley' in the United States, running from Texas in the south to Nebraska in the north – do get more twisters than others. But tornadoes actually appear quite regularly on every continent in the world, barring Antarctica.*

The good news is that the vast majority of tornadoes aren't killers. Most don't even cause much damage beyond a few broken tree branches and toppled chimneys.

Tornadoes are measured on the Fujita scale (named after Tetsuya 'Ted' Fujita, the Japanese professor who created it),

---

* Which is almost a shame, as an Antarctic tornado would at least give penguins a chance to see what flying is like.

which goes from 0 to 5, based on the amount of damage the twister does. F0 and F1 ('weak') tornadoes snap branches, peel off roof tiles and shift cars around in driveways. F2 and F3 ('strong') twisters uproot trees, topple trains and tear roofs off houses like lids off yogurt pots. By the time you get to F4 and F5 ('violent') tornadoes, you get flying cars and farm animals. You also, occasionally, see houses lifted right off the ground, then broken into pieces that land hundreds of metres away.* Which, among other things, *really* confuses postmen.

Perhaps not surprisingly, F4s and F5s cause most (roughly 67%) of the deaths and injuries associated with tornadoes. But thankfully they're also *by far* the rarest type of tornado, which keeps the flying-house traffic down to a happy minimum.

The chances

The odds of dying in a sandstorm or snowstorm are, for most people, very low indeed – perhaps 1 in 1,000,000. Of course, if you're crossing the Sahara or Gobi Desert by camel, or trekking through the Himalayas, then your odds are a lot higher. But then, if you're the type of person who does those kinds of things, you're either very well prepared, or you're that SAS 'survivor' bloke on the telly. (And if things go bad for him, he can always eat the guy with the camera.)

---

* Or, if you're called Dorothy and you're in the movie *The Wizard of Oz*, it might deposit you, your dog and your entire house into another dimension – surprisingly all in one piece.

Tornadoes are a bit easier to stick a number on. Of the 1,000 or so tornadoes that strike the US (the most twister-prone region of the world) each year, only 1% are F4 or F5 'violent' ones, and that low percentage seems to hold true for the rest of the world too. As with lightning, your chances of being hit by a tornado also depend on where you live. The average odds of experiencing death-by-twister sit at roughly 1 in 60,000, but are quite a bit lower outside tornado-prone regions.

The lowdown

Sandstorms and snowstorms are dangerous, but fairly predictable. You may never see one in your little part of the world, and, even if you do, they're not so hard to deal with if you're properly prepared.

Tornadoes, however, are famously unpredictable, and there's no real way to 'deal' with them apart from getting out of the way or hiding somewhere safe. To that end, people who live in areas where twisters are common often build underground storm shelters, or take cover in the basement of the house when a tornado warning is sounded. It's also important if you live in a 'twister zone' to keep an emergency survival kit handy (with food, torch, radio and first-aid box) in case you get trapped inside the house. The most important thing, though, is simply to stay aware of what's going on with the weather, so you know if it's likely that a storm will bring tornadoes along with it. That means checking the TV and radio weather reports whenever there's a storm around. Meteorologists (scientists who study weather patterns) can predict where and when tornadoes are likely to appear just by watching for spinning cloud patterns within storms. And although they're not always right, it pays to listen to them, just in case!

Scary as all this sounds, there is a happy ending. Thanks to improvements in weather-forecasting methods and communication by TV and radio, the number of deaths caused by 'killer' tornadoes has been dropping steadily in most parts of the world. In the US during the 1950s, 18 tornadoes killed more than 18 people each. In the 1980s, only 2 tornadoes killed that many, largely thanks to the better warnings and information people were receiving by then. So while twisters can be fearsome, we don't need to feel too afraid of them if we understand them and do the right things. If you're still not sure what these things are, check out my handy tornado guide below:

Torna**D**o's and Torna**D**on'ts

Do

☺ Listen for tornado warnings on TV and radio during storms.

☺ Prepare an emergency kit, just in case.

☺ Take cover in the basement if a tornado is coming.

Don't

☹ Listen to your iPod or watch *Twister* on DVD.

☹ Prepare your hang-glider.

☹ Sit on the roof with your digicam and try to get some good shots for YouTube.

The wrath of Katrina

On 29 August 2008 Hurricane Katrina, one of the most devastating hurricanes of all time, slammed into the southern coast of the United States. Over the next two days it tore through Louisiana, Mississippi, Alabama, Tennessee, Kentucky and Ohio, leaving a trail of floods and damaged buildings 125 miles wide. Worst hit was the port city of New Orleans, where winds hit speeds of over 125 mph, and floodwaters surged over the protective barriers north of the city, leaving 80% of it underwater and destroying over 200,000 homes.

All told, Katrina did over 125 billion dollars' worth of damage, eclipsing Hurricane Andrew's 21 billion-dollar wrecking spree in 1992, and making it the single most destructive hurricane in recorded history. Yet in terms of human losses, neither could compare to the Galveston Hurricane of 1900, which killed 6,000–12,000 people and completely destroyed the coastal island of Galveston, Texas. Of this, one Galveston reporter said that the events of 8 September 1900 'could never truly be written. As for many, no words could ever be spoken again about the deadly hurricane that reshaped the Gulf coast forever'.

The fear

Screaming winds topple trees and buildings all around. Floodwater fills your house and drowns you inside, or sweeps you off the street into a huge, gushing river filled with mud, silt and debris. Being caught in a superstorm must surely be one of the most terrifying experiences you can imagine. Most of us have seen news reports showing the effects of recent typhoons and hurricanes in Asia and the Americas. If regular thunderstorms are scary, then superstorms are super-scary.

The reality

Tropical storms – and their larger cousins, typhoons, hurricanes and cyclones – are no joke. The average hurricane measures around 340 miles across, and releases more energy in 24 hours than all the power plants on the planet put together. To make matters worse, superstorms like these bring with them a hat-trick of dangers: winds of up to 150mph, high waves and storm surges, and flash flooding caused by heavy rain.

Storms, Cyclones and Hurricanes

Storm: a disturbance in the Earth's atmosphere that affects its surface – usually through strong winds, heavy rain, and possibly thunder, lightning, ice, snow or hail. They can be light, moderate, severe or extreme, depending on the wind speed.

Cyclone: organized, rotating storm system that forms over tropical or sub-tropical waters. There are various types of cyclone, which are given different names depending on which ocean they form over. To be a true cyclone, the wind speed must be over 69 mph.

Tropical Cyclone or Cyclonic Storm: a cyclone which forms over the Indian or south-west Pacific Ocean.

Typhoon: a cyclone which forms over the north-west Pacific Ocean.

Hurricane: a cyclone which forms over the Atlantic or north-east Pacific Ocean.

OK, now for the bright side. Only about one-third of the tropical storms and cyclones that strike land each year are what we'd call major storms, or storms in categories 3, 4 or

5 on the Saffir-Simpson hurricane scale. These are storms with wind speeds of over 110mph, and are the ones that commonly destroy buildings and cause dangerous flash floods. The majority of tropical storms fall in categories 1 and 2. These have winds between 74 and 100mph. So they're still very powerful, but they usually do little more than fell trees, break windows and flood roads. In the last 100 years, there have been only a handful of category-5 storms, so the worst kinds of superstorms are fairly rare.

Even if a major storm does hit, the winds rarely knock down entire houses, and with proper hurricane-proof windows, shutters and roof supports on your house, wind poses little danger to anybody inside.

The real danger comes from the heavy rains, storm surges and flooding. These do pose a real threat, and tend to cause almost all the deaths during major storms. So that's where you need to act fast in order to stay safe. Tropical storms and hurricanes are enormously powerful, but they're also huge and fairly slow-moving, so they're reasonably easy for weather forecasters to spot and track. The best way to avoid the dangers of a hurricane is simply not to be there when it hits. If you pay close attention to weather reports and leave at the first sign of trouble, there's nothing even a superstorm can do to harm you.

The chances

The odds of being killed in a superstorm (including being struck by the hail, lightning and tornadoes that accompany it, or drowning in floodwaters) are roughly 1 in 50,000. Again, this varies a bit depending on whether you live near the coast or inland, and whether or not you live in an area prone to hurricanes and typhoons (like the south-eastern US or south-western Japan). But the real risk has more to do with how much information about approaching storms you have access to, and how quickly you can evacuate if you need to. With a good advance warning and plenty of time to escape, you can reduce your odds of being hurt in a superstorm to almost zero.

The lowdown

Superstorms will probably always be a threat to people living in many areas of the world. But although they might regularly destroy buildings and property, they can be spotted, tracked and avoided by people, given enough of a warning. Storm-tracking radar and computer software are becoming more powerful and accurate all the time, and armed with the knowledge they give us, we can beat a respectful retreat from superstorms without having to live in fear of them. As with other types of natural disaster, you can also prepare for the worst by strengthening your house, preparing an escape route, and putting together an emergency survival kit – just in case you're unable to get away from the house in time. With all this done, your odds of being harmed by a superstorm go from 'very low' to 'extremely low', and you can feel confident and prepared rather than anxious and afraid.

LOON ENTERS TYPHOON

I experienced my first superstorm in Japan in September 2000. I had moved to Japan in July of that year, just one month before the official 'typhoon season' – the two months when most of the typhoons happen – began. Growing up in England, I'd never really experienced a hurricane or typhoon before. (There was a small category-1 hurricane in Kent when I was 12 years old, but I slept right through it, and woke up confused to find my parents walking around with candles because the power was out!) So when this first typhoon hit the city of Tsukuba, where I was out food shopping that afternoon, I completely underestimated it. As I emerged from the shopping centre, hundreds of Japanese shoppers were gathered by the door, afraid to go outside as the wind roared past. 'It can't be that bad,' I thought. 'Besides, I have to get this ice cream home before it melts.' So, ignoring the other shoppers' protests, I pushed past them and stepped out into the typhoon. Bad move.

Tables and chairs from a nearby cafe whipped past my head. Bolts of lightning struck things within a hundred metres of where I staggered and leaned into the wind. I got less than half a mile away from the shops before the deafening thunderclaps scared me into a sprint, and I ran (still trying to keep hold of my shopping bags) to shelter in a nearby hotel. A uniformed security guard inside called to me and pulled me into the hotel lobby: *'Gaijin-san! Hayaku! Kochi! Kochi!'* ('Quick, Mr Foreigner! In here! In here!'.) He must've thought I was a complete loony.

I waited there for an hour and a half while the typhoon passed, then finally set off on the rest of my journey home. As I neared my apartment block, I found a pair of my pants lying damp and sodden in the road. Then another. Then a T-shirt and a single, lonely sock. All mine. Unfortunately I'd left all my washing out to dry on the balcony of my third-floor flat, and the typhoon had helpfully distributed it all over my neighbourhood.

Oh well. At least I still had the ice cream . . .

Mount St Helens explodes

'At 8.32 a.m. on 18 May 1980 an earthquake of magnitude 5.1 occurred directly underneath the volcano. This was the trigger for the enormous eruption that quickly followed in its wake. Within a few seconds, the entire north flank of the mountain exploded, creating one of the most gargantuan* rock and debris avalanches of all time, advancing at a speed of 60mph. Within seconds, the temperature in the danger zone had soared to over 280°C. Snow and ice on the peak of Mount St Helens melted instantly, creating raging torrents that poured down the slopes into the valleys, destroying all life in their path.'

The fear

Smothered, burned and melted by a river of red-hot lava. Crushed inside a crumbling building, or thrown into a deep crack in the earth beneath your feet. Flattened and drowned

---

* If you haven't seen this word before it means 'really, massively, hugely enormous'. As opposed to the massively, hugely annoying 'ginormous', which isn't a word at all, and really bugs me. Why glue 'gigantic' and 'enormous' together, when either one can do the same job just fine on their own? Might as well say 'egantic'. Pah!

by a colossal tidal wave.* Not many of us have experienced an earthquake, tsunami or volcanic eruption – but not many of us would want to either. The deadliest earthquake on record killed over 830,000 people in Shaanxi, China, in 1556. And in 2004 the deadliest tsunami on record killed over 225,000 people in Indonesia, Thailand and Sri Lanka.

As for volcanoes, about 50 or 60 erupt *every year*. Half of them just spew molten lava down their sides, while the other half actually explode – sending out huge, deadly clouds of gas and rock, and raining down lava bombs and thick, suffocating ash for miles around.

Scary? Errr ... yes.

The reality

Volcanoes are essentially holes in the Earth's outer crust, through which red-hot, molten rock (magma) from the liquid layer beneath can escape. If the molten rock oozes its way out gradually, you get bubbling lava-flows, and the cone of a volcano is built up from layer upon layer of this stuff setting hard atop itself. But if the route to the surface becomes blocked by hardening magma, it 'caps' the volcano,

---

* Not that 'tidal waves' have anything to do with tides at all. They're caused by earthquakes or (every 100 million years or so) asteroid strikes. Another *egantic* failure to use the right words. Oops. Now *I'm* doing it. Let's stick with the term 'tsunami'.

and pressure can build up beneath until it eventually blows its lid. This is what happens during a volcanic eruption.

An erupting volcano is an awesome and hellish sight, and you certainly wouldn't want to be anywhere near one when it goes off. Just ask the people of Pompeii, Italy, who until AD 79 lived on the sides of an active volcano called Mount Vesuvius. When Vesuvius blew, it buried the town in clouds of burning ash, leaving little behind but statue-like impressions of the poor townspeople and their pets.

Now, you might think to yourself, 'Why would anyone want to risk living on the side of a volcano in the first place? The people of Pompeii were just asking for it, weren't they?'

Well, as it happens, the soil around volcanoes tends to be very rich in nutrients and ideal for farming, so many towns and villages have been built on the slopes of volcanoes to take advantage of the fertile ground. And as risky as this 'extreme farming' might seem, the people who choose to live this way know something else about volcanoes too – that the chances of actually being killed by one drop steadily *the further you are away from the crater*. And while you may think, 'Great – then I'll stay at least a thousand miles away, thanks!', for many volcano-dwelling farmers, the risk is worth the reward. Here's how it works.

At less than 100m from the crater, you're in the death zone. Here you have extreme temperatures, mini-earthquakes, landslides, toxic gases and virtually no chance of survival in the event of an eruption. So staying here for long pretty much guarantees you'll be toast.

At 100–300m away, you've got roughly a 50% chance of surviving an eruption, provided you're not hit by the pyroclastic cloud – a plume of boiling gas and rock that explodes out of the crater at temperatures up to 800°C. If that happens, you may have the rare honour of being vaporized – turned into a gas – yourself.

At 300m–10km away, you're still at risk from lava bombs and mudflows, but your odds are getting better. Particularly if you're good at dodgeball and swimming.[*]

At over 10km away, you're actually reasonably safe. Although lava-flows may travel further than this (up to 100km or more, on occasion), lava isn't, believe it or not, that much of a danger to people at all. It usually moves very slowly (2 or 3mph/3–5km per hour), so you can walk backwards faster than it flows towards you. Look at it that way, and it doesn't seem quite so scary, does it?

As for earthquakes, they're a bit different. Earthquakes are caused by floating plates (called tectonic plates) of the Earth's crust grinding past each other. All the continents and oceans of the world sit atop these vast plates, and in turn, they sit (or rather 'float') atop a sea of molten rock in the mantle layer beneath. The plates and the land masses on top of them are constantly moving. We usually don't notice this, because they move too slowly for us to feel it. Except, that is, during an earthquake.

During an earthquake, the grinding plate edges (plate

---

[*] OK – this is a lie. No one's *that* good at swimming. Or dodgeball.

boundaries) can become temporarily stuck or caught against each other. Pressure and strain build up between the two surfaces – until eventually the tension breaks and the plates jerk free. This sudden jolting movement creates the massive vibration that we – sitting on the landmasses above the plates – experience as an earthquake.

The good news is that while small earthquakes are very common (about 8,000 per day!), on average we only get one very large quake (scoring 8 or more on the Richter scale) each year, worldwide. Also, the big, damaging quakes almost always happen in specific, predictable areas – on the boundaries between the floating tectonic plates we were just talking about. Some regions (like Japan, Indonesia, northern India and the west coast of America) sit right on top of a plate boundary, so get more than their fair share of large earthquakes. Other regions (like northern Europe, Australia, and central Africa and America) sit right in the middle of a plate, so they get very few. So depending on where you live, you might not have much to fear from earthquakes at all.

Tsunami are almost always caused by large earthquakes, but are rarer still. They happen as an undersea earthquake sends a sudden ripple of motion upward through the water from the ocean floor. This ripple lifts a vast ridge of water above the sea surface, which then collapses into a series of immense waves that grow larger and larger as they approach shallower depths near land.

They're also only really a threat to people living in low-lying coastal areas or islands, and if you live far enough inland (or up high enough) they won't really affect you. And even in the areas that are threatened, the prediction and warning networks for tsunami have improved a lot in recent years. This now gives people more of a chance to escape in the interval between the earthquake and the wave hitting land.

The chances

The odds of being killed by a volcanic explosion, lava-flow or associated mudslide are about 1 in 80,000. Obviously they're much higher if you live right on the side of a volcano, but, on the flipside, if you live *nowhere near* a volcano, your odds of being killed by one pretty much drop to zero.[*]

The average person stands a 1 in 130,000 chance of dying in an earthquake, and only a 1 in 500,000 chance of being killed by a tsunami. Again, this changes a lot depending on where you live. But for most people in most places, it's highly unlikely that you'll be hurt by either one.

The lowdown

If you live very close to a volcano, close to a plate boundary or on low-lying coastline in a region known for earthquakes, then you need to be aware of the risks and

---

[*] Unless, that is, a massive *supervolcano* like the one under Yellowstone Park in the USA blows. Then we could all be done for. But thankfully that only happens about once every million years or so. The last supervolcanic eruption was about 75,000 years ago, so we should be fine for a little while (or 925,000 years) yet. Phew!

dangers of eruptions, earthquakes and tsunami. Just as with hurricanes and tornadoes, a little preparation and planning can go a long way towards keeping you safe in the event of a disaster. Usually this just means knowing how to get to a safe place quickly and having food, water and emergency supplies ready in case you're trapped or stranded.

But if the place where you live doesn't fall into one of those three categories, then you have little (if anything) to fear from these three forms of natural disaster. Thankfully, geologists and engineers have learned a lot from past earthquake experiences, allowing us to build more earthquake-proof buildings in cities and towns near plate boundaries. These structures are designed to bend and sway during an earthquake, rather than crack and crumble. So if you live in one of these, there's far less chance you'll become trapped or injured inside. We've also become a lot better at monitoring plate boundaries and volcanoes for signs of trouble, which helps us to predict (although far from perfectly) where and when earthquakes, eruptions and tsunami are likely happen.

Sure, it's possible that a large earthquake might happen right in the middle of a plate . . . that a tsunami might travel further across the ocean and further inland than usual . . . or that an unknown underground chamber filled with magma might erupt without warning and form a new volcano in your hometown. All of these things are possible. But the chances of them actually happening are so small that they're basically not worth worrying about at all. As we'll see in the next section on asteroids and comets, some things have such frighteningly huge consequences that they're hard to ignore. Yet once you know the massive odds against them, ignoring them is exactly what you can and should do. Volcanoes, earthquakes and tsunami are big and scary, certainly. But if they still freak you out, just ask yourself: what are the odds?

Fear Facts:

Volcanoes can be classified as *active, dormant* or *extinct. Active* volcanoes either erupt regularly or still show signs that they might erupt again – like swelling, shifting or regular earth tremors. *Dormant* volcanoes have been quiet for at least 10,000 years, and *extinct* volcanoes are unlikely ever to erupt again – usually because their underground lava supply has been cut off.

There are about 40 known *supervolcanoes* in the world. These are volcanoes which have produced particularly (and frighteningly) large eruptions in the past – eruptions big enough to blast out a crater 40 or 50 miles wide and affect the entire

Earth's climate as exploding gases enter the atmosphere.

Almost all supervolcanoes are extinct. The last one to blow was Mount Toba in Sumatra, roughly 75,000 years ago. That eruption was *ten thousand* times more powerful than the Mount St Helens eruption in 1980.

EARTHQUAKE EMERGENCY! (OR MAYBE NOT)

Not long after my first typhoon experience in Japan, I soon had the pleasure of my first real earthquake. I was sitting in an Internet cafe, emailing a friend back in Scotland, when the earthquake hit the building (well, it actually hit the whole city and surrounding area – but you know what I mean). It started with a gentle rumbling and rocking of the room, and I thought at first it was maybe just a big lorry going by. But then the rumble got bigger. The floor, the walls, everything started shifting from side to side, practically scaring the pants off me. I mean, like most people who didn't grow up in earthquake-prone regions, I'd always kind of taken it for granted that floors and walls ... well ...

stay put. Take it from me – it's very unnerving when they suddenly decide not to.

Jumping out of my seat, I quickly scanned the room to locate the exits. 'But wait,' I thought to myself. 'Should I make a run outside to the car park, duck under the desk in case the ceiling falls in, or what?! And what about everyone else in here? They don't seem to be going anywhere. So should I grab them and help them outside too? . . . or . . .

'Hang on a minute. Nobody else is getting up. They're just sitting there. They're still TYPING!! In fact, they don't look bothered at all . . .'

So, very slowly, and keeping an eye on all the Japanese emailers around me who seemed so unafraid of the continuing earthquake, I sat down again, and continued my email.

'Heiyyy mate,' I typed, trying hard to hit the right letters as my fingers skidded about on the keys, 'therre seems to be amn esrthqiuake goiung onn. Nobosy else seems botherdd tho' . . .'

It was the first of many earthquakes I'd experience during my two years in Japan. None of them did anything worse than tip bottles, glasses and books off shelves, and although none of them turned out to be dangerous, it took a long time before I stopped freaking out whenever they happened. The weirdest thing was suddenly waking up in the middle of the night, and wondering why you were awake . . . then feeling the gentle rumble and rocking of the earthquake's aftershock.

A 'second sun' falls on Siberia

'We were sleeping. Suddenly we both woke up at the same time . . . We heard whistling and felt strong wind . . . We started crying out for father, mother, brother, but no one answered. There was noise beyond the hut, we could hear trees falling down . . . then the thunder struck . . . This was the first thunder . . . The earth began to move and rock, wind hit our hut and knocked it over . . . Then I saw a wonder: trees were falling, the branches were on fire, it became mighty bright . . . how can I say this, as if there was a second sun . . . my eyes were hurting, I even closed them . . . And immediately there was a loud thunderclap. This was the second thunder. The morning was sunny, there were no clouds, our Sun was shining brightly as usual, and suddenly there came a second one!'

Tungus tribe witness, 1905

The fear

On 30 June 1905, an asteroid or comet exploded 5 miles above Tunguska, a remote forest area in Siberia, Russia. The words above come from a witness to the event, a child of one of the Tungus tribes that lived in the area. Although no one is known to have died from it, the Tunguska fireball flattened 1,200 square miles of forest, and was the largest asteroid or comet impact in recorded history. But that's not to say that bigger ones hadn't gone before . . .

The Tunguska asteroid was just 60 metres across, yet it exploded with the force of 1,000 atomic bombs. A strike from an asteroid ten times larger would cause earthquakes, throw up enough dust into the atmosphere to blot out the Sun, and kill millions of people worldwide. If it were ten times larger again (about 6,000m/4 miles wide), the explosions, earthquakes and firestorms that followed would most likely make us extinct, along with most other species of life on the planet. This is called an Extinction Level Event (or ELE), and it's thought that this is what killed most of the dinosaurs – along with 75% of the Earth's other species at the time.

If an asteroid or comet of that size hit us again, we'd have nowhere to run, nowhere to hide. We'd be done for. No question. So in the grand list of things to be terrified of, surely this has to come near the top, right? Right?

The reality

You probably didn't know this, and you might not believe it, but huge rocks from Space are thumping into the Earth's atmosphere *all the time*. And not only do they regularly fail to wipe out the human race, but most of them go completely unnoticed.

Unless, of course, you're a star gazer. Or, better yet, a *shooting*-star gazer. That's because space rocks measuring less than a few metres across usually burn up in the atmosphere, causing pretty, flashing meteor trails – also known as shooting stars. If they're a bit larger, they might cause small, temporary fireballs that disintegrate long before they hit the ground. And while a huge planet-killing fireball *is* a truly terrifying thing to think about, asteroids hundreds of metres across (and capable of causing an ELE) don't strike the Earth very often at all. If they did, then we probably wouldn't even be here, as it would've been difficult for life on Earth to get a foothold with pesky fireballs destroying most of it every thousand years or so.

The last *really* big one was probably the same one that finished off most of the dinosaurs. It struck the Earth around 65 million years ago, and the chance of one *that* big hitting us again within the next century is less than one in a million. The same goes for comets, which are more or less the same thing as asteroids, only they're more ice than rock.

Of course, some rocks do sometimes make it all the way down to the ground (those ones we call *meteorites*).

Even some pretty large ones. So there is an outside chance that one of these might crash through the ceiling of your house while you're in the bath, or drop out of a blue sky while you're out for a relaxing stroll. But the chances of one falling *right where you are at the time* are incredibly small, so smaller meteorites don't pose much more of a threat to you than their larger asteroid cousins.[*]

The chances

In all, the odds of being killed by a falling space rock (including meteorites, asteroids and comets) during your entire lifetime are between 1 in 200,000 and 1 in 500,000. This is regardless of where you live, or how much time you spend looking up in an effort to dodge them. This also makes space rocks – believe it or not – one of the *least* hazardous natural disasters around, so they're not really worth worrying about at all!

The lowdown

The odds of being struck, individually, by a single falling space rock are so small that most people rightly ignore the possibility of it – in much the same way as they ignore the possibility of a satellite, an aeroplane, or an unlucky skydiver falling on them.

---

[*] As a space rock, you don't get to be called an 'asteroid' unless you're at least 30 metres wide. So I imagine there are lots of very miffed 29-metre rocks out there in Space, who probably still tell all their mates they're 'asteroids, really'.

These things seem so unlikely they're almost funny to think about. But massive, planet-killing asteroids are different. When you hear about them, they conjure up images and words – explosion, firestorm, extinction – that may trigger a real emotional response (changes in heartbeat and breathing, sweating, and so on) in your body. With *that* comes the feelings of dread and fear. And suddenly the risk of being killed by an asteroid seems many times larger than it actually is. But the risk hasn't changed – only how you're thinking about it.

Asteroids and comets are a perfect example of how our emotions can get in the way of our logic and reason when it comes to things we're afraid of. In effect, the emotional part of the brain decides how good, bad, safe or scary something is before the logical part even gets a look in. So you're left feeling really afraid of something, yet you can't really explain to someone else exactly *why that is.*

One way to break this fear cycle is to start to look at the same scary things in a new way. Weighed up against other nasties, asteroids and comets are so unlikely to affect you at any time within your lifetime that it's better to think of them as 'never gonna happen' and be done with it. Then, chances are, the Earth will keep spinning through Space largely unbattered by anything too big, and you can take relaxing strolls and baths without wearing a crash helmet.

Fear Facts:

- There are over 100,000 known asteroids in our solar system, including 2,000 that are classed as Near-Earth Objects (or NEOs), which pass through the Earth's orbital path, and have the possibility of hitting us one day.

- In fact, a 60m asteroid called 2009DD45 whizzed past the Earth on 2 March 2009, missing us by 40,000 miles. That might seem pretty far off but, in terms of Space distances, it's actually a close shave.

- Over 12,000 asteroids have been named, and if you spot a new one, you're allowed to name it yourself!

3 Doctors, Dentists and Deadly Diseases

Scary Stories

Ever heard a horror story about an evil nurse who terrorizes people with her needles and instruments, or a dentist who seems to love causing pain?

How about news headlines like: 'Killer Bug Ate My Face' or 'New Flu Could Kill Millions'? Chances are, you've seen or heard one of these at least once within the past year.

And barely a week goes by without there being some kind of food-poisoning scare in the news. Beef is laced with deadly *E.coli* bacteria. Chicken and eggs give you *Salmonella*. It's enough to make you avoid going anywhere – or eating anything – ever again!

But if all these stories were really true, then surely we'd all have been done for a long time ago. Every week, stories like these appear in newspapers, on TV and on the Internet. Yet we keep on going to the doctor and dentist, going out, eating food and breathing air – all with few signs of these killer people and bugs we hear so much about. So what's going on?

One simple answer to that question is that many of these stories (such as the ones your mates tell you about doctors and dentists) are exaggerated or completely made up.* But they can't all be lies. I mean, newspaper and TV reporters can't just make things up and get away with it, can they?

Well, not exactly. But it's important to understand that newspaper reports, TV programmes, books and movies all need to have stories in order to be interesting. So the people that create them tend to choose subjects that will make good stories. That means something with good guys, bad guys, danger and drama. And 'killer bug' stories fit that formula perfectly.

So when some innocent, unsuspecting person some-where is killed by a rare nasty virus – or a rare case of food poisoning – then it makes great material for news reports, and the same stories get repeated over and over again. Un-fortunately for us, this tends to give us the idea that killer

---

* One of my mates in primary school once told me that a dentist had actually *killed* him the day before. I stared at him for a few seconds until he realized what he'd just said. He stared back. Then he added, 'Well – he didn't *kill me dead*, obviously. I mean, I got *better . . .*'

bugs and food poisoning are a lot more common (and a lot more dangerous) than they actually are.

This is because our brains weigh up how risky things are partly by using *memory*. If we can remember recently being bitten by a snake, poisoned by a dodgy egg, or burned by a hot kettle, then our brains make us react carefully (or even fearfully) when we next encounter snakes, eggs and kettles. But if the bite, burn or bout of food poisoning happened a long time ago – and we've safely dealt with snakes, eggs and kettles plenty of times since – then we gradually forget about these 'dangers'. With enough time and experience, we even begin to relax around them or ignore them completely.

The trouble is, our brains don't fully separate out *the things we hear from someone else* (or the things we see in newspapers, on the Internet, on TV and in the movies) from *the things that actually happen to us*. So whenever you see or hear a story about an evil dentist, or a TV report about a 'deadly' virus or 'poisonous' egg, the brain files this idea in the form of a memory, which your brain may refer back to later on as if it was real.

Little by little, your brain starts to get the idea that killer dentists, viruses and foods are all around you and killing people all the time! Your brain takes no notice of the fact that *you've never actually been harmed* by a dentist, virus or food. Nor does it note that the dentist story may have been exaggerated or made up, or that the reports were about *rare* viruses and *rare* batches of poisoned food.

So the next time you go to the dentist, or encounter

the 'killer' food, or someone sneezes near you on a bus, your brain refers to these false memories and kicks off an automatic fear response. You don't notice this happening, but it does. All you know is: 'Dentists are evil,' 'That egg might kill you!' and 'That gross snotty guy on the bus might have bird flu!'

But the truth is that doctors and dentists aren't deadly, everyday germs aren't vicious killers, and real 'killer bugs' are so rare in the world that they aren't much of a danger either.

In fact, bacteria and viruses are all around us, all the time. And as long as we stick to a few simple steps in dealing with them, we certainly don't need to flinch from every patch of dirt or airborne snot-droplet that we encounter.

So without further ado, let's dive into the icky world of medicine and microbes . . .

Fear Facts:

Although people often get them mixed up, bacteria and viruses are very different things.

- Bacteria are tiny living organisms – the simplest forms of life on the planet. Each bacterium is a single living cell, which feeds, grows, and splits itself in two in order to reproduce. These two 'daughter' cells then split again and again, creating a colony of organisms. They live pretty much everywhere on the planet, inside and outside our bodies.

Viruses are not considered to be true living things, as they cannot feed, grow and reproduce by themselves. Smaller and simpler than bacteria, they consist of a small strand of DNA (or a related chemical called RNA) surrounded by a protein coat. Viruses pass into living cells (either bacteria, or those of other organisms) and hijack the cell machinery to copy themselves.

Antibiotics work on bacteria, as they stop bacterial cells from growing or reproducing. Antibiotics don't work on viruses, as they have different structures and ways of reproducing to bacteria. So there's no point taking antibiotics for a cold or viral infection.

Dirt, Grime and Bacteria

World of germs

Right now, whether you know it or not, you're surrounded and under attack. A vast, invisible army of bacteria is all around you, ready to strike from every possible angle.

Sitting outside on the freshly mown grass for a picnic? Every gram of soil beneath you contains over a billion bacteria, of over 10,000 different species. Going for a swim in the sea? The salty water contains up to 200,000 bacterial cells per litre. And if you think your house is spick and span and bacteria-free . . . think again. The average home boasts 3.2 million bacteria per square inch of toilet bowl, 18,000 bacteria per square inch in the kitchen sink, 300 per square inch on the telephone, and 200 per square inch on every light switch.

The fear

Germs, or bacteria, cause disease by attaching themselves to us and gaining entry to our bodies. They crawl in through our eyes, ears, noses and mouths. They squeeze through cracks and cuts in broken skin to enter the tissues and blood vessels beneath. They even hitchhike on dust particles and water droplets floating in the air, and are sucked deep into our lungs with almost every breath. Once inside, they breed. They divide, multiply and *party*. They squeeze water and nutrients from our cells, they travel around the body in the bloodstream, and they make us ill in any number of different ways.

Since bacterial germs thrive in dirt and filth, the *fear of dirt* and the *fear of germs* go hand-in-hand, and we give them a single name – *mysophobia*. True *mysophobics* will do anything to avoid getting dirty or contaminated by germs. They'll stay indoors to avoid the 'filthy' world outside, open doors with their elbows, and wash their hands up to fifty times a day in an effort to stay germ-free. But with over five million-trillion-trillion bacteria on the planet (that's a five with 30 zeros after it), there really is no escaping the big, filthy, world of germs . . .

The reality

It's true – like reality TV programmes, germs are everywhere, and there's no getting away from them. But for the most part, we don't need to, as few of them do us any harm. Over 95% of the bacteria on the planet are completely harmless. Which is how all of us (and I mean *all* of us, not just the stinky ones who don't wash) can carry *trillions* of bacteria around with us every day without even noticing them.

Staphylococcus bacteria cover your skin and line the insides of your nose and mouth. Your stomach lining harbours millions of rod-shaped *Lactobacillus* bacteria. Your guts contain billions of *Escherichia coli* (otherwise known as – gasp! – the dreaded *E.coli*). And that's just for starters. They live in your teeth, on your tongue, under your fingernails, up your bum* . . . pretty much anywhere you can imagine. What's more, they live there for your entire life. Yet none of them (usually) do you any harm at all.

That's because they've evolved to live with us, and we've evolved to live with them. They've adapted to thrive at our normal human body temperatures, and to feed happily on bits of undigested food, dead skin cells and other things we don't need. Our bodies hold them in check by using the skin and gut lining as a barrier, keeping them outside the body or inside the long food-tubes of the digestive system. This stops them getting into the tissues and bloodstream where they could do us harm.

And if they make it past that first line of defence, our immune cells race in to provide reinforcements. White

---

* So the next time you complain that the place you live isn't much fun, just think: it could be worse – you could be a bacterium.

blood cells and antibodies that find bacteria in the tissues or bloodstream surround them and summon help from other cells – cells that punch holes in bacteria and digest them. Like an army of microscopic bouncers or security guards, immune cells use the invading bacteria's outer coating as ID, and clone thousands of copies of 'memory' cells that recognize that ID – just in case that type of bacterium tries to get in again. Clever little things, those immune cells.

But why make it all so complicated? I mean, why don't our bodies just kill off all the bacteria there are and be done with it?

Well, for starters that'd be no easy task, since (as we've seen) bacteria are everywhere in our environment, all the time. So it'd be an enormous waste of energy to try and kill off *all* the bacteria we come into contact with, just to get at the few among them that might do us any harm. Instead, by keeping a layer of harmless bacteria around, our bodies use the 'good' bacteria to keep out the 'bad' ones. The trillions of harmless bacteria that already live on us (and inside us) out-compete most of the would-be settlers that might do us harm – by eating all their food, and stopping them from getting a toehold on our bodies.

Also, many bacteria are actually incredibly helpful to us in hundreds of ways. We use them to make foods, drinks, vaccines, antibiotics, fuels, pesticides and more. As a matter of fact, we wouldn't even *be* here without them, and we couldn't go on living without them either.

Bacteria were the first forms of life on the planet, and they evolved billions of years before we did. They spent billions of years altering the Earth's atmosphere by sucking up methane and carbon dioxide and spewing out oxygen. If they hadn't been there and done that, then none of the big, oxygen-breathing animals on the planet – including us – would ever have developed and survived. Even now, bacteria continue to remove carbon dioxide from the air and oceans. This helps provide the very air we breathe, and also helps protect us from the effects of global warming. Pretty helpful for a bunch of 'killer' bugs!

The chances

Of course, bacteria and viruses can and do kill people. Common infections picked up from the environment cause an average of 35 deaths per country, per year. In some places it's much higher, in others much lower. And your chances of picking up an infection depend, of course, not only on where you go, but also what you do there. If you go for a swim in an open sewer, or roll around with your mouth open in the grassy 'dog-walking' area of your local park, then you're far more likely to pick up harmful bacteria.* But just hanging out in the average home, garden, beach, meadow, public building or park, you're very unlikely to

* Not sure why you'd want to do this, unless perhaps your dog has real trouble learning the 'roll over' command and you're trying to demonstrate it for him. In any case – bad idea.

be made ill by bacteria – provided you follow a few basic rules (see below). Follow these rules, and your basic chance of being killed by a common infection drops to below 1 in 1,000,000.

The lowdown

It's pointless wasting energy trying to avoid contact with germs, as a) you don't need to, since most germs are harmless, and b) it's absolutely impossible to do, anyway!

Besides that, trying to keep your body and environment too sterile (say, by using antibiotic soaps or too much disinfectant around the house) might actually weaken your immune system by stopping it from being exposed to bacteria. Remember, your body's immune-cell 'bouncers' need to ID the 'bad guys' to recognize them and protect you in future.

If you want to protect yourself against bacterial and viral infections, then these few basic rules should be more than enough:

- Wash your hands after using the toilet, and before eating. This prevents you from transferring harmful bacteria from your hands to your mouth, where they may be swallowed.
- Avoid picking your nose or biting your fingernails. Apart from being gross, these are great ways for bacteria and viruses to hitchhike their way into your body on a grubby fingertip.

If the defensive barrier of your skin is broken by a scratch, cut, graze, burn or animal bite, always clean and disinfect the wound to stop bacteria sneaking in through the gap.

Beyond that, you needn't worry about random germs getting into your body, as millions of years of evolution have already done all the worrying for you. Your immune cell 'bouncers' are waiting at the doors, and if the bugs aren't invited to the party, they're not staying for long.

Fear Fact:

Bacteria live in every known environment in the world. Some live their whole lives floating in the atmosphere, while others have been found living more than 1,500m underground. Some survive year-round in Arctic ice, at temperatures as low as −85°C. Others live inside volcanic vents in the deepest parts of the ocean, at temperatures above 106°C.

Micro-monster

We've all eaten something that 'didn't agree', with us. Perhaps it was a dodgy sausage left out too long in the chip shop or a dodgy yogurt left too long in the fridge. Most of the time we get away with a sore stomach and a quick sprint to the toilet. But pity the poor person who eats food containing the bacterium *Clostridium botulinum*. When this little monster disagrees with us, it *really* disagrees with us. It normally lives in soil, but when it finds its way into the human body through foods (usually vegetables) it causes complete havoc.

The *botulinum* toxin is the most powerful poison known to man. It paralyses nerves and muscles, stopping you from speaking, swallowing and (eventually) breathing. One gram of it could kill a million people, and less than a nanogram (0.000000001g) is enough to kill a single child or adult. If there was ever a great excuse for not eating your vegetables, this is it! But since the bacterium is easily killed by washing and cooking – and eating your vegetables is better for you than skipping them – your mum is unlikely to agree. Sorry.

The fear

We all have to eat, and most of us do so at least three times per day. That means eating more than 70,000 meals over the course of a lifetime, any one of which could contain a microorganism that makes you horribly ill. Some of these 'food bugs' just make us feel tired or sore for a few hours. Others make us vomit and poo explosively (sometimes both at the same time). The very worst of them can paralyse and kill us, and judging by the high number of news reports we see about these, that must happen a *lot*.

Listeria lurks menacingly in cheese, *Campylobacter* camps out in tainted meats and milk, and *Salmonella* sits waiting in everything from chicken to eggs to chocolate. Food poisoning strikes millions of people every day, all over the world.

But if we have to eat to live, then what do we do when our food is trying to kill us?

The reality

Don't worry – our food isn't really trying to kill us,[*] and neither are most of the bacteria that live in it. As we saw in the last section, less than 5% of the bacteria around us (including those living in or on our food) are actually harmful, thanks in part to the strength of our immune systems.

But it's true that some bacteria can and do cause us harm when we swallow them, and roughly 1 in 3 of us will become sick with food poisoning at one time or another in our lives. In the USA alone, around 76 million people get food poisoning each year, and these millions are matched (or topped) on every other continent (except perhaps Antarctica, where there simply aren't millions of people to get it!). Thankfully, the vast majority of these 'poisonings' turn out to be pretty mild, rather than the 'deadly' outbreaks we hear so much about in the media.

E.coli, for example, is usually a harmless bacterium, and billions of them live in our guts already. Millions of people eat *E.coli* along with their food every day, and never even realize it. The only problem comes when a rare and dangerous type (or strain) of the bacterium turns up, like the

---

[*] Except, perhaps, for *fugu*, the poisonous pufferfish eaten in Japan. That one really is trying to kill you. Specially trained chefs are supposed to cut out the poison glands before they slice and serve it, but every year at least a few people drop dead after eating 'dodgy' ones. I ate *fugu* once, without realizing what it was. Luckily I'm still here to report back on how it tasted: good, but not so good I'd risk my life by eating it twice!

0157:H7 strain that causes most of the '*E.coli* outbreaks' you hear about in Europe and North America. This particularly nasty strain makes a toxin called the *shigatoxin*, which causes vomiting and diarrhoea, and can be fatal. But this strain is quite rare (less than 1.5% of all food-poisoning cases involve it), and what's more, 90–95% of people who become ill with it survive.

The truth is that while food poisoning is pretty common, serious illness or death caused by food poisoning are pretty rare. And if you treat your food properly, by storing and cooking it carefully enough, then food poisoning is totally avoidable and nothing much to worry about.

The chances

The odds of getting food poisoning differ between different countries. In the developing world, over 1.8 million people are killed each year by microorganisms in food or water. In parts of Africa and Asia food poisoning is a common cause of death. But these tend to be places without good water treatment, without good sanitation (sewers and waste-removal systems), and with poor hospitals and healthcare. In developed countries like the US, UK and Australia, far fewer people are killed, although still probably more than there should be – between 400 and 5,000 per year. But all in all, your chances of dying of food poisoning are still very low – probably around 1 in 3,000,000.

The lowdown

Food poisoning is common enough to be a real danger, but as long as you follow a few simple rules in storing, preparing and eating your food, it's still nothing to be afraid of. Take care with your food and you can enjoy it fear-free for life.

Keeping food fresh and safe is all about preventing bacteria from growing in it, or killing them off if they already have grown. So . . .

- Make sure you store your fresh foods properly, keeping them in the fridge, or (if you're keeping them for longer) freezing and defrosting them as needed.
- Remember that chilling and freezing don't usually *kill* bacteria, they just stop them from growing so fast. This is why your food still 'goes off' in the fridge eventually, so keep track of how long things have been in there by checking sell-by dates and labels. This is also why you shouldn't 're-freeze' things once defrosted – bacterial spores can survive the first freeze and multiply when they're thawed, so the second time you thaw the food it could be swarming with bacteria within minutes of defrosting.
- Make sure foods that need to be cooked – like meat and eggs* – are *fully* cooked before you eat them. That means heating them right through to kill all the bacteria

---

* It is possible to eat raw (or rare) meats and eggs, of course. But unless they're VERY fresh, you're always at risk of food poisoning. So if you're in any doubt at all, it's better to cook 'em up and show the bugs no mercy!

inside, not just heating up the outside and leaving the middle bit lukewarm (this is especially common with fast-cooking microwave ovens, so beware!). Check the food packaging for guidelines. Once cooked, eat the food immediately, or store it as if you hadn't cooked it at all, as even within a few hours more bacteria from the air can settle and start to grow back.

If you're eating raw foods like sushi, make sure they're ultra-fresh so that bacteria haven't had hours to grow on them before you eat them. Also, keep raw and cooked food separate when preparing meals, to prevent bacteria from being transferred from one to the other. And always wash your hands after handling raw food, to avoid ferrying bacteria from your fingers to cooked foods later on (or straight into your mouth!).

Finally, if in doubt, throw it out! If something looks or smells dodgy, then it probably is. Much safer to discard it and let the bacteria grow in the bin, rather than swallow it and see what happens in your stomach!

HOW TO EAT IN REVERSE
(WARNING: GROSS-OUT ALERT!)

When I was little, I was a terribly picky eater. My mum had serious trouble getting me to eat vegetables, and chicken, beef and fish had to be in the form of nuggets, burgers and fingers before there was any guarantee I'd scoff them.

But after university, and just one year of living in Japan, all my picky eating habits went out of the window. I was eating all kinds of raw and cooked vegetables, and I discovered that I really liked sashimi and sushi (cuts of fresh raw fish served on their own or on top of lumps of sticky rice). These fresh, raw foods had more flavour to them, and I gradually became more and more brave and experimental with the things I ate. After the raw fish came raw shrimp, raw crab, raw jellyfish and raw sea cucumber (which is a long warty sea worm, not a vegetable). One of my favourite things was a thin cut of nearly raw beef called *shabushabu*. To kill off the bacteria, you just swiped it twice through a dish of boiling water, then popped it in your mouth. It was juicy, tasty and delicious.

Then one evening, I went out to dinner with some of the other teachers from the school where I was working. They all ordered *namatori*, which is, basically, small chunks of raw chicken plopped on top of a bowl of rice. But I wasn't convinced.

'Raw chicken?' I said, 'won't that make you sick?'

'No, no,' answered my friend Makoto,* 'It's very fresh. Like sushi. It's very good!'

---

* This is the same guy who fed me the poisonous *fugu* pufferfish. You'd think I'd have learned my lesson . . .

So, trusting in my new 'iron stomach', I ordered up my own bowl of raw chicken chunks, and (trying to ignore the fact that it looked very much like a bowl of cat food), I scoffed it down. The next day my body decided to teach me a painful lesson about bacteria and raw meat.

Some forms of food poisoning make you throw up for hours, until your head spins and it seems like the bottom has fallen out of your world. Others leave you stranded on the toilet for hours while the whole world – ahem – seems to fall out of your bottom. This one did both.

By the end of it, I was lying in a hospital bed, dizzy and several pounds lighter, hooked up to a drip of salty fluids and vitamins through a needle in my arm. None of my friends had become sick from the *namatori*. They were immune, it seemed, to the bacteria which had so successfully attacked my guts for the previous 24 hours.

I still love Japanese food, and I happily eat raw fish all the time. But I draw the line at raw chicken. Unless you want to find out what it feels like to be a bubbling fountain of body fluids, I suggest you do the same . . .

Needle nightmare

I counted down the days on the calendar with increasing dread. A month before the jab, I imagined it as a thin, sharp, three-inch needle being stuck into my shoulder, making me yelp in pain as the nurse pushed the plunger thingy down. A week before the jab, the needle had grown in my thoughts. Now it was six inches long and looked like a steel drinking straw, and it made my whole arm go dead as the nurse cackled and jabbed it in. An hour before the jab, sitting in the doctor's waiting room, the day-dream had become an epic horror movie. The needle was over a foot long and wider than a pencil, the doctors and nurses held me down as they speared my arm with it . . . and I screamed as a gushing fountain of blood sprayed into the air and over their crazed, laughing faces. Yaaaaaaggghhhhhh!!!!'

The fear

When you think about it, *aichmophobia* (pronounced: ayk–), or the fear of needles, is a pretty logical and reasonable fear to have. It's basically a fear of being stabbed by a stranger with a sharp, pointy object. And who in their right mind wants that?

Then you have dentists, who wield not only needles, but also drills, pliers and a whole host of shiny, glinting instruments of torture. There you lie, with your mouth propped open in silent (or at best, grunting) protest, while the dentist sets about scraping, drilling and pulling at your chompers with wild abandon. Little wonder, then, that *odontophobia* (the fear of dentists) comes in ahead of needles in the list of common fears.

And finally, you have doctors and nurses – the objects of *iatrophobia*, or the fear of doctors. They peer and poke at your ears, eyes and throat, seeming to find all the sorest spots in the course of examining you. Worse yet, they can send you to hospital, where surgeons might slice you open on the operating table, chop out your tonsils, and goodness knows what else.

What if you woke up in the middle of it all? What if the surgeon was out to get you? What if all doctors, nurses and dentists were a bunch of nutters – evil maniacs using their needles, drills and scalpels as weapons? It's all enough to *make* you feel ill, if you aren't already!

The reality

All right – stop that. Needle injections really aren't that bad, and doctors and dentists aren't out to get you. While some needle, doctor, and dentist phobias begin with one-off bad experiences (like a particularly nasty tooth extraction, or being hastily prodded by a gruff and impatient* doctor), most do not. Most come from those all-powerful scary stories we hear from news reports, movies and other people. Our friends exaggerate stories about injections** and trips to the hospital to make them sound more impressive, dramatic and interesting. And where there have been one or two doctors over the years who have hurt or killed people, news stories have been focused only on these rare 'bad apples', and not on the thousands of good, caring doctors and nurses out there.

To make things even worse, if you are anxious about visiting a doctor or dentist, your fears can also build and amplify while you wait for your appointment to come around.

Ever sat in a doctor's or dentist's waiting room sweating, fidgeting, and generally dreading what might happen when you finally get in there? If so, then you already know that fear doesn't always hit you all at once. It can come as a sudden

---

* And after all, what good is a doctor without patience? Geddit? Doctor . . . patients? Oh, forget it.

** As an example of this – the injection story at the beginning is mine. Although the *actual* needle turned out to be tiny (and didn't hurt at all), when all my friends heard the story, it was more like the bloodbath detailed here. I probably created a few *aichmophobes* with that story.

shock to your system, or it can build and swell inside you, turning from dread to panic, little by little. Which one is worse? Well, that depends who you ask.

Some people say they hate shocks and surprises, so being pounced upon and eaten by a snarling tiger that appears from nowhere is just about the scariest thing they can think of. But now imagine that you knew that in two days' time, at exactly 10 a.m., you would be attacked and eaten by a snarling tiger, and there was nothing you could do to avoid it.* Would that make you feel better, or worse? Some people might say 'better', since knowing about the tiger would help you to prepare for the shock. But would it really help? And how could you prepare for what you know will be a terrifying experience – one that you can't possibly avoid?

For many (if not most) people, knowing about the tiger wouldn't help at all. Right after you were told about it, you'd picture the scene, and begin to worry. At first, this worry (or *anxiety*) wouldn't look like much from the outside – maybe a wrinkled brow, tense neck or shoulders, and slightly quickened breathing. Then, as the hours passed, the anxiety would turn into *stress*, as your brain would react to your tense muscles and fast breathing by assuming you were in trouble and might soon need to run or fight. To help you do this, your brain would then trigger the release of chemicals called hormones into your bloodstream, where they quicken the heart rate and direct blood away

---

* Even clunking about in a full suit of armour, or locking yourself in a tiger-proof cage all day.

from your digestive system and towards your muscles. This would make your muscles even more tense, your breathing even quicker and shallower, and your stomach queasy and nauseous.

Right about now, you would start noticing these signs yourself, and you'd decide that if all this is happening, you must be *really* scared. Then you'd get more and more anxious and panicked as your body seemed to spiral out of control. Eventually, this cycle of think-react-think-react might build into even bigger physical changes and reactions, like trembling, sobbing and crying. This is how fear builds up in cycles and stages, from 'slightly worried' to 'totally losing it'.

No one wants to be eaten by a snarling tiger. It would be terrifying. Dreadful. But knowing about it in advance would only give you more time to feel all this terror and dread before it happened.

A similar thing can happen when waiting for anything you believe will be scary or unpleasant, including getting an injection from a doctor, having a tooth pulled by a dentist, or your tonsils removed in hospital. The difference is that none of these things (trust me) are anywhere near as bad as being eaten by a tiger. In fact, most injections, tooth-pullings and operations are quite painless, and nothing to worry about at all.

Injections, for example, are usually done with pretty tiny needles – just a few centimetres long and less than a millimetre wide. The reason why some jabs (like the BCG jabs you get as a teenager to protect against tuberculosis) leave scars is because of a reaction between your skin and the vaccine, not because the needle scarily massive!

What about dentists? Well, during the course of a visit they may scrape, drill, fill, remove or fit braces to your teeth. But with a good dentist and a good anaesthetic, you probably won't feel much except a bit of pressure against your head.

Doctors, meanwhile, may use their fingers to prod at sore spots (to check for inflammation and internal damage), and may use instruments like a *stethoscope* (the cold, heart-listening thing), *otoscope* (the thing they peer into your ear with) or *opthalmoscope* (the eye-examining gadget). But none of these instruments or tests really hurt. Afterwards, you'll probably be given some medicine and sent home, but even if you are sent to hospital for surgery, most operations don't hurt either. The *anaesthetist* will numb the body area or put you to sleep while the surgeon works, and you'll wake up the next day missing your tonsils (or appendix, or whatever), but otherwise feeling just a bit sore.

Most of the fear involved in medical phobias comes from not knowing (or being misled about) what really happens when you 'get in there'. Once you know what to expect, you can control your anxiety and stop it before it builds up into real stress, fear and panic. What's more, most nurses, doctors and dentists will even help you to do this by telling you what to expect, and reassuring you about it all as you go along.

The chances

The odds against a standard injection, examination or dental operation going wrong and causing you permanent harm are millions to one. As for hospital operations, they may have different risks depending on what needs to be done (tonsil and appendix removals are very common and safe, while kidney and liver transplants are more risky).

But look at it this way – the odds of becoming seriously ill because you *avoided* an injection, examination or operation are far, far higher. Nurses, doctors and dentists are there to heal you, not harm you. So you're best off seeing them whenever you need to, and letting them do their jobs.

The lowdown

Vaccinations, blood tests and other needle 'jabs' are nothing at all to be afraid of. The needles are too small to do any real damage, and most feel more like a 'pinch' than a 'stab'. So no matter what tall tales your friends might tell you about them, there's really no need to panic about getting a jab. If nothing else, a quick pinprick is far less painful and dangerous than catching the actual disease the jab is trying to prevent, as we'll see in the next section . . .

Doctors and dentists are nothing to be afraid of either. They're there to help, so you should trust them and talk to them rather than live in fear of them. Doctors may have to prod and poke you a bit to properly diagnose what's wrong with you, but they certainly won't hurt you on purpose. In fact, doctors are trained to be sensitive to your pain and your worries, so if you're uncomfortable or afraid, just tell them, and they'll help you through it.

Dentists, too, are trained to be sensitive and to avoid causing you unnecessary pain. Most dentists are so good at this that they can drill and remove teeth without you even feeling a thing. Instead of drilling and scraping, they may use special air abrasion tools – which blast the tooth with a mixture of air and powder at high pressure – or even use lasers to do painless dental work. Most dentists can also give painless injections, by using tiny jabs above the gumline (where you can hardly feel them) to numb an area. And if you *do* need a bigger injection, they'll often do a couple of these smaller ones first, so that you don't feel the 'big one'. If you're *really* afraid of needles and injections, the dentist may even use anaesthetic gels or patches instead.

So if your dentist is hurting you, he shouldn't be – find a new one! Trust me, there are loads of nice doctors and dentists out there. You just have to give them a chance, and be a little patient.* Now say 'ahhhh...'

THE PAINFUL PATH TO WISDOM (TEETH)

Everybody has wisdom teeth – the pairs of molar teeth which sit right at the back of your upper and lower jaw. But some people go their whole lives without them ever poking their way through the surface of the gums, while in others they barge through and press so painfully against your cheeks and other teeth that they have to be removed right away. And being the largest of all the molar teeth, they often don't come out without a fight.

When I was about 16 years old, the pair of wisdom teeth in my lower jaw decided to make an appearance. First the left one, then the right. The one on the left wasn't painful at all, but the one on the right was scissoring into my cheek and causing a lot of pain. So off to the dentist I went.

Two hours and several anaesthetic injections later, I emerged from the dentist's with my face and tongue numb and my gums throbbing. The tooth had, unusually, cracked in half during the operation,

---

* Or a big patient, if you're taller. Heh-heh-heh. Oh, wait – I've already done that gag...

so the dentist had to dig out the rest like he was mining for gold. 'Hope I don't have to do *that* again!' I thought. And since the other one seemed fine, I thought I'd got away with it.

But two years later, 'Ol' Lefty' decided he wasn't happy, and began cutting painfully into my other cheek and barging into my other teeth like an unwelcome party guest. Remembering my last tooth-tunnelling experience, I put off going to the dentist as long as I could. But eventually the pain just became too much to bear, and off I went.

Lying back in the chair, I explained to the dentist (a different one this time) how bad it was with the 'last one', and how I really wasn't looking forward to what was coming next. While numbing up my gum with injections, she told me she understood completely, and chatted to me about TV and movies while she continued to prod and probe at the tooth with an assortment of blunt metal instruments.

'Do you want to keep it?' she asked suddenly.

'Keep what?' I said.

'Your tooth,' she answered.

'Probably not,' I said mournfully. 'I think I'm going to want to forget about it once it's done. Just let me know when you're about to start pulling, so I can prepare myself, OK?'

'Too late,' she said. 'It's done.' And, incredibly, she waved the tooth in front of my face, clamped between what looked like a pair of nutcrackers!

'Eh?' I said. 'What?'

'It's done,' the dentist replied, smiling. 'Do you want it or not?'

'Errr . . . OK. S'pose so . . .' All that fuss over nothing! I was almost disappointed. Almost . . .

That was the day that I lost a chunky wisdom tooth but gained this chunk of wisdom: Don't fear the dentist – just get yourself a nice one!

A most horrible way to go

The Ebola virus is one of more than 18 types of virus that can cause the horrifying disease haemorrhagic fever. Want to know how horrible? OK . . . but unless you have a very strong stomach, I would skip this bit if I were you . . .

Haemorrhagic fever starts with a sore throat, chest pains, a skin rash, and diarrhoea. Then your blood fails to clot, your skin starts to bruise, and your spleen, kidneys and brain begin to swell up. Next you start bleeding from the eyes, nose and mouth. Finally, just before you slip into a coma and die, you vomit a thick, black sludge of blood and disintegrated internal organs.

Ouch!

The fear

Haemorrhagic (or 'bleeding') fevers like Ebola are truly the stuff of horror movies. Liquefied organs, horrible skin sores, explosive bleeding . . . on a long list of things you don't ever want to experience, I would definitely put Ebola right at the top. Then there's the famous flesh-eating MRSA bacterium. Since first making news in the late 1990s with the 'Killer Bug Ate My Face' headline, it has popped up in news reports at least once or twice a year. It seems that somebody, somewhere is always getting their face eaten off, and it's only a matter of time before the hungry, monster bug finds its way to you . . .

The reality

Face-eating bugs and organ-liquefying viruses are perfect horror-movie material, and they make very dramatic stories for news reports, novels and feature films. But they're actually very rare, and very few people are affected by them each year. Being stories, these books, films and reports very often also exaggerate how nasty the bug is – leading us to think that these diseases are everywhere, that we could catch them at any time, and that when we do . . . we're in for an inescapable grisly end.

But in the real world, Ebola has never been seen anywhere outside of a few villages in west Africa, and certainly not anywhere in the developed world, where people seem so terrified of it. In the last 20 years, only three people in the UK, USA and Russia – all laboratory workers – have been infected, and all after accidental jabs with needles. And two of those survived.

Even in the countries where Ebola outbreaks have

happened – such as Uganda, Gabon and the Republic of Congo – it only causes between 10 and 200 deaths per year. That may sound like a lot, but it's nothing compared to the millions that die each year of diseases like tuberculosis and malaria.

Part of the reason for this is that most forms of Ebola aren't very contagious, so don't spread nearly as easily as the movies and news reports would have you believe. And grisly as it sounds, the *really* contagious forms of Ebola kill people so quickly that no one has time to leave and seek help, so the virus rarely spreads far beyond the village where an outbreak begins.

As for the 'new, infectious, flesh-eating bacteria', they're neither new nor infectious nor actually flesh-eaters at all! The bacterium that causes the 'flesh-eating' disease (otherwise known as *necrotizing fasciitis*) is quite a common one, called *Staphylococcus aureus* (or SA). It lives on your skin and in your nose, and the worst it usually does is cause (quite harmless) skin or throat infections, which are easily cleared up with a course of antibiotics. The problem comes when the strain of SA you catch becomes resistant to methicillin and other antibiotics normally used to treat these infections. Then it becomes what's known as Methicillin-Resistant Staphylococcus Aureus, or MRSA. This is the so-called 'flesh-eating bug'.

But MRSA doesn't actually 'eat flesh', it just releases toxins as the infection develops, which sometimes break down the skin and soft tissues around the infection. When this happens, what starts with a pimple can – if left untreated – turn into a blister or a hole. In a few rare cases, it can lead to more serious (and deadly) infections of the lungs, heart and brain. But it doesn't actually *eat* your flesh. And more often than not, the simple, pimple-like infection clears up on its own and leaves you totally unharmed.

The chances

Outside west Africa, the chances of catching a deadly form of the Ebola virus are next to zero, and even in Africa, your chances of catching it are pretty slim. As for the 'flesh-eating' MRSA bug, it affects elderly people far more than it does others. (This is partly because they have weaker immune systems, and partly because they tend to be in hospital more often, so have more opportunities to catch it.) But still, even for people over 85, the chances of catching a deadly MRSA strain are about 1 in 1,000, which is still pretty low. For everyone else, the chances are about 1 in 1,000,000, or small enough to ignore completely.

The lowdown

As with many of the other health scares we hear so much about, being bombarded with scary stories about killer bugs and viruses gives us the impression that they're both more common and more dangerous than they really are. Ebola and MRSA are dangerous, as they can both cause deadly diseases. But nasty as they are, they're still very rare, and are nowhere near as infectious or powerful as the news reports and movies make them out to be.

In the disaster movie *Outbreak*, Ebola spreads around an entire country in days, travelling through the air and infecting whole cities full of people at once. In reality, the Ebola virus can't survive for long in the air, and even if it did cause a country-wide outbreak, it would probably mutate very quickly into a less dangerous form before it had a chance to do *that* much damage.

In news reports about MRSA, reporters often say the bug is 'resistant to all antibiotics', and 'can't be treated', when in reality most MRSA infections can still be treated and cured with the antibiotic vancomycin, and other treatments are being developed as we speak.

So don't believe everything you see on TV, in newspapers or on the Internet. Killer bugs aren't about to attack you, and your face will most likely stay un-eaten for life.

Fear Facts:

Ebola is in the family of viruses known as **Filoviruses**. 'Filo' means 'thread' in Latin, and they get this name because, close up, each viral particle looks like a little loop of string. Stringy 'filo' pastry gets its name for the same reason . . .

but is obviously far safer to eat than Ebola.

Ebola is related to the rabies virus, which is technically more deadly – since rabies kills 100% of those it infects, while Ebola kills 'only' 90%.

Another name for Ebola is Green Monkey Fever, which makes little sense, since green monkeys don't actually exist.

Worse than war or plague

In 1918, the last great pandemic (or whole-world outbreak) of the influenza virus killed between 25 and 50 million people across the globe. It killed three times as many people as the whole of World War I, which had only just ended. In fact, more people died of influenza in those nine months than in all four years of the bubonic plague – the famous 'Black Death' that swept through Europe in the 14th century. And the next flu pandemic could happen at any time . . .

The fear

Viruses like the one that caused the 1918 'Spanish Flu' outbreak are still with us, lurking in birds and other animals and just waiting for the chance to mutate and start infecting people. The influenza virus is particularly sneaky, as it changes its outer appearance by mutating every time it infects a new host. This makes it one of the hardest viruses for the body's immune system to recognize and fight off, and also makes it almost impossible to fight with vaccines.

By the time you create a vaccine against the current form of the virus it has already changed, so the vaccine probably won't work. So, with no working vaccine and no cure, a new form of influenza could sweep the planet again just like it did a century ago. The 1918 virus infected around a fifth of the world's population (which at the time was about 1.8 billion) and killed millions. If that happened again – in today's world of over 6.7 billion people – more than 1.3 billion would be infected worldwide. That's about equal to the entire population of China, or twice the population of Europe. Yikes!

The reality

Those are some scary numbers, and the truth is, a new strain of flu really *could* sweep the world and infect that many people. But don't panic! Once again, we're only getting one side of the story . . .

The panic about bird flu (or *Avian Influenza*, as it's known to virologists, or scientists who study viruses) comes from the fact that this strain of flu changes (or *mutates*) extremely quickly, making it almost impossible to vaccinate against. This also makes it very deadly to the animals it infects, as their immune systems have so little time to mount a response before it changes its outer coat to look like something else.*

Wild birds can carry the Avian Influenza virus in their guts without getting sick, but when it passes to

---

* This is a bit like the virus putting on a wig and one of those glasses-nose-moustache disguises. 'Nahh – I'm not Flu,' it says to your immune cells. 'I'm Dave. You know – Dave Harmless, from down the road. No need to worry about me . . .'

domestic birds like ducks, geese and chickens*, they often become sick and die. If that was the end of the story, there wouldn't be much of a problem. Every year some farmers would lose a few flocks, but beyond that, no danger. The trouble is, sometimes the virus can mutate so that it can infect humans too. And when it does, it very often kills them. Influenza viruses that have 'jumped' from birds to people have so far killed over 300 people in parts of south-east Asia, west Africa and the Middle East, and every year the number of people infected seems to be growing.

But this doesn't mean bird flu is about to infect the whole world. In all of the human cases seen so far, the virus was caught directly from an infected bird or from contact with bird droppings. (Part of the reason why these infections are happening is because people in those places keep live birds

---

* Which I suppose might give you one good reason for being *alektorophobic* (see page 5) after all.

in crowded markets and in their homes, making it easy for the virus to spread to people. You can't get bird flu from eating chicken

This is important, because it means the 'bird' virus hasn't mutated into a 'human' one, so can't yet be passed *between* humans. Phew!

So at the moment this flu virus is still a *bird* flu that can infect people who live closely with birds, rather than a *human* flu set to spread around the globe in coughs and sneezes. Which means you don't have to worry just yet about catching deadly flu strains from that snotty guy at the bus stop, or that kid who sits behind you and keeps coughing on you in class.[*]

The chances

Scary and threatening as it seems, the chances of your catching bird flu right now are so small that it's hardly worth thinking about. Even in south-east Asia, where the most cases of bird flu have been found, the odds are as low as 1 in 4 million. In Europe, the US and most other places there have been no cases of bird flu found in humans at all. Here the odds are more like 1 in 100 million. That makes 'death by bird flu' the least likely thing in this book to happen so far!

---

[*] Although this still isn't too cool, and you should probably ask him to cover his mouth anyway. You might not get bird flu from him, but you might catch a common cold or – at the very least – a big, wet blob of phlegm on the back of your neck. Mmmmmm, nice.

The lowdown

For now, bird flu is only a threat to bird farmers, and even then it's more of a threat to their wealth than it is to their health. And while 300 people infected over the last few years might sound like a lot, it's almost nothing compared to the 500 million people infected with 'regular' human flu each year, the vast majority of whom survive. So bird flu, at the moment, is hardly even a dot in the bigger picture of world diseases.

Of course, there's always the chance that Avian Influenza *could* mutate into a strain which can jump between humans – and if that happens there could be another pandemic like the one in 1918. But it hasn't happened yet, and it may not happen within our entire lifetimes.

If that doesn't make you feel much better, then try this: if a new flu pandemic was to happen, we'd almost certainly be a lot better prepared to battle it than the world was nearly a century ago. Even without a 'bird flu' vaccine, we've learned so much about the spread of diseases and how to treat viral infections since then that we would most likely save millions more lives. Back in 1918, we'd barely got the hang of radio broadcasts. Nowadays, news spreads around the world in an instant via satellite signals and the World Wide Web. So governments across the globe can work together to limit the spread of disease through quarantines, instantly share information about new viruses as they arise, and airlift medical supplies and doctors in a matter of hours.

Of all the 'scary, deadly' diseases that make it into media reports every month, bird flu is, in reality, probably the worst of the bunch. But the new flu pandemic is not here yet, and if we're lucky it may not come at all – at least not in the way it did back in 1918. In the meantime, scientists and governments are keeping an eye on flu outbreaks in every corner of the world . . . just in case. So when the flu comes again, it'll have to face a global self-defence force. Next time, hopefully, we'll be ready for it.

MY FRIEND WHO HAD THE PLAGUE

In my final year studying science at university, my classmates and I all spent months in the laboratories, day after day, working on the experiments and projects that would lead to our final grades. I worked with antibodies and DNA fingerprints, spinning samples in high-speed rotating centrifuges and carefully placing bits of invisible DNA into tiny wells and plates. Others worked with bacteria and viruses, spreading tiny amounts of them on to dishes coated with sugary gels, and growing them in incubators until the small, round colonies appeared. We'd all work hard on our experiments during the day, and then meet up in the canteen at lunchtime to scoff sandwiches and chat.

One girl, Claire, sat on the bench opposite me

in the lab, but I noticed that few people sat with her down in the canteen at lunchtime. So one day I plopped myself down next to her and asked what she was working on.

'Yersina pestis,' she said. 'I'm finding out how it reacts to antibiotics.'

Ah. Now it all made sense. Suddenly, I didn't want to be sitting next to her either.

Yersina pestis, you see, is a bacterium. A bacterium that causes a disease. A very, very, nasty one, more commonly known as *bubonic plague*. You might know it from the history books, as it caused the Black Death in 14th century Europe.

'Errr . . . isn't that, like . . . a bit . . . you know . . . dangerous?' I asked, while coughing on my half-swallowed lump of sandwich. I'd been working less than six feet from this girl for weeks, and suddenly I started wondering if that new zit on my shoulder might be something else . . .

'No, not really,' she said. 'It's not that contagious. It's fine, as long as you're careful with it.'

And she was right. Believe it or not, plague isn't that contagious. Unlike a cold or flu virus, the bacterium that causes it can't survive long in the air, so it's difficult to get it from breathing or touching an infected person. Back in the 14th century it killed millions of people by hitch-hiking in insects – fleas – which lived on the rats that swarmed through the cities of Europe.

Still, I decided to finish my sandwich elsewhere.

'See you later, Claire,' I said, as I got up to leave. 'Oh, and err . . . good luck with your plague.'

'Yeah, thanks,' the plague girl replied sullenly.

4 In the Unlikely Event

Weighing Up the Odds

When trying to understand your fears, it's usually not good to think about *that one thing you're afraid of* and nothing else. In fact, that's a sure way to make it seem bigger and scarier than ever. Instead it helps, if you can, to try to look at scary things in a different way – to see them in the 'big picture' of nasty possibilities so that you can understand them in perspective.

Of course, we've already been doing this for every fear we've looked at so far. Every time we look at 'The chances' of a scary thing happening and try to put a number on it, we are, in a way, ranking or scoring it against all the other scary things in the book. But so far, most of the fearsome things we've looked at have had pretty low odds of occurring. Shark attacks, asteroid strikes and death-by-face-eating-bug all have odds against them of thousands – or even millions – to one. Most of us look at numbers like these and think something like this: 'A million to one? That means it's *never* going to happen.'*

That, in a way, is fair enough. But as the numbers get smaller – 1 in 10,000, 1 in 1,000, 1 in 100 – our minds tend to start 'ramping up' the chances, until we feel like the odds of something happening are much higher than the numbers are actually telling us. This is because the human brain isn't really very good at weighing up probabilities and chances.

Don't believe me? OK, let me give you a little test.

Let's say I have a coin. The odds of it coming up heads or tails when I flip it should be the same: since there are only two possible outcomes, then the chances must be 1 in 2 for each outcome. Right?

OK, now let's say I flip it four times. The first time, it comes up heads. The second time, heads. Third time . . . heads. And the fourth time . . . heads again. Now, which outcome do you think is more likely on the next throw? Is it a) tails, b) heads again, or c) dunno, seems like they're equally likely to me.

If you're like most people, you answered a). After all, it's come up heads four times already, hasn't it? Five heads in a row has got to be less likely than four heads and a tail.

---

* Unless we happen to be playing the lottery, when we think, 'That one in a million could be me!' Funny how the mind works, innit?

The true answer is c). It doesn't seem right, does it? But it's true. Five heads in a row has the exact same probability of happening as four heads followed by a tail. Or five tails in a row, for that matter. Every time you flip the coin, there's a 1 in 2 (or 50%) chance of it coming up heads, and an equal 50% chance of it coming up tails. And it doesn't matter how many times you flip the coin, those odds never change. Over 1,000 tosses of the coin, the results will tend to balance themselves out, giving somewhere near (but not exactly) 500 heads and 500 tails. But over just five tosses of the coin, getting five heads (or five tails) is actually quite likely, and you or I shouldn't be surprised when it does happen.

But we are surprised, because our brains didn't evolve to weigh up probabilities, and our intuitions – or gut feelings – tell us that 'five heads in a row' must mean 'he's got a trick coin with two heads on it or something'.[*]

OK, now let's try something else. When you're looking at the numbers involved in plane crashes, you might come across a pair of facts like this:

💥 The chances of dying in an aeroplane crash are about 1 in 4 million.
💥 Each day, worldwide, around 4 million people travel by aeroplane.

---

* Which could also be true. So avoid betting money on coin flips with anyone who does magic tricks as a hobby.

Looking at these numbers, you might immediately think: 'hang on a minute – that means somebody somewhere dies in a plane crash every day!'

But that's simply not true. Fatal plane crashes (as we'll see) are actually very rare. It's just that your head is messing with you again. Like the odds of the flipped coin turning up tails, every time you fly the odds of crashing are roughly the same. For the coin, the odds are 1 in 2; for the plane, the odds are 1 in 4 million. So while it *seems* like taking that one flight puts you at real risk of being that '1 in 4 million passengers who won't make it off the plane', this simply isn't the case. In reality, the average person would have to take a flight *every day* for *thousands of years* before they could expect to find themselves in a crash.

Knowing all this, of course, doesn't simply kick the brain into understanding, or remove all your fears in a puff of brainy logic. As we've seen, the brain doesn't quite work that way when it comes to fears. No matter how smart and well-armed with facts and numbers you are, the emotional bit of the brain can still kick in and drown out all your lovely logic and clever probabilities with a single sweep of powerful body responses (tense muscles, sweaty palms, racing pulse) that make us scared all by themselves. So to get around your fears, facts and numbers alone aren't enough. You still have to work on understanding your own emotions and feelings.

Still, getting things in perspective is a good way to start. Especially with scary things – like plane crashes – which seem very likely, but really aren't. On the flipside, it also helps us realize how things that seem perfectly safe, like crossing the road, can actually be more dangerous than flying.

Now, I bet that's got you really worried . . .

Smashed on the runway

In March 1977 the worst airline accident in history happened on the Spanish island of Tenerife. Two jumbo jets collided on a foggy runway, killing 583 people in the double wreck.

'As the American plane continued taxiing down the runway, the departing KLM (Dutch) plane suddenly appeared out of the fog. The aircraft was accelerating down the runway at a speed of more than 125 miles per hour. Both pilots tried to accomplish the impossible: the American pilot turned his airliner sharply to the left at full thrust in an attempt to get off the runway, and the Dutch captain forced his plane off the ground in an attempt to fly over the American aircraft – but it was too late ... The two planes collided, and soon the runway was covered in debris, all of it on fire. Nine hours would pass before the inferno was finally brought under control.'

The fear

Pteromerhanophobia,[*] or the fear of flying, is extremely common. If you don't have it yourself, you almost certainly know someone among your family or friends who does. (I can count six pteromerhanophobes among my lot!) Studies have shown that over half of all children and adults are frightened or anxious at least *sometimes* when they fly. And it's fairly easy to understand why.

There you are, hurtling through the air in a huge metal tube weighing hundreds of tonnes over which you have no control. You know it's *supposed* to be safe, but the more you think about it, the more it seems that *this thing really has no business being in the air at all.* All that's between you and the treacherous pull of gravity that could bring you crashing back to earth are a few rumbling engines and about 30,000 feet of thin air. You start to sweat as you stare out of the windows. If that wing cracks, you think to yourself, we're doomed. Or if just one of those engines cuts out, we'll be plummeting from the sky

---

[*] And if you think *that's* a long word, then check *this* one out: Hippopotomonstrosesquippedaliophobia. Believe it or not, that's the name for the fear of long words. After reading that monster, I think I might have it too . . .

into a fiery wreck on land, or plunged into the cold, dark ocean, trapped in a mass of twisted metal . . .

The reality

You've heard it before, you'll hear it again, and you still may never really believe it . . . but plane crashes really are extremely rare events. Especially when you consider how many flights take off and land safely worldwide every day.

Over 4 million people a day travel by plane, which adds up to over *1.7 billion passengers* on over *25 million flights* per year. Of these, there are only a handful of crashes each year – in some years, none at all. And although airlines based in western Europe and North America account for over two-thirds of all the planes in the sky, less than a quarter of crashes happen on these flights. Typically there is only one crash per year, and often there are no crashes at all. What's more, most accidents happen to poorly maintained planes in developing countries, and we probably wouldn't even hear about them if they didn't make such dramatic pictures and stories for world news reports. So once again, 'scary stories' are partly to blame for our fears. Being bombarded with these stories makes us think plane crashes are more common and more of a danger to us than they really are.

In fact, thanks to improvements in aircraft design, pilot training and air-traffic-control technology, flying has become safer than ever over the last few decades. While the total number of flights each year has been steadily increasing, the number of fatal crashes has stayed roughly the same – which, if you think about it, means that an *increasing* number of flights are arriving *safely* each year. More planes, more flights, but fewer crashes per flight.[*] Which is nice to know.

The chances

The chances of your particular flight ending in a fatal crash depend a little on what kind of plane you're flying in, and which airline you fly with. Believe it or not, *large* planes like jumbo jets have *better* safety records than small propeller planes that seat far fewer people – partly because they're more stable in flight, and partly because they're checked so thoroughly before they're allowed to take off. Among the airlines, some have perfect safety records, without a single fatal crash in millions of flights, while other airlines have a number of crashes to their name.

That said, even the 'worst' of these (like Cubana Airlines and Air Zimbabwe) only have an average of one crash in every 18,000 flights. Most airlines have 'crash rates' of between 1 in 2,500,000 and 1 in 5,000,000. In all, the chances of any one person being in a fatal plane crash average out at around 1 in 4,000,000 – about 50 times less likely than being struck by lightning, and about 8 times less

---

[*] That's the total number of flights divided by the total number of crashes each year, **NOT** the number of times each plane crashes on a single flight. You wouldn't catch me on a plane if we had to calculate *that!*

likely than being killed by an asteroid impact.* How's that for weighing up the odds?

The lowdown

The numbers tell us that flying really is nothing to be afraid of, yet fear of flying is incredibly common. This is partly because our brains don't listen to numbers alone, and partly because many people who think they're afraid of flying are actually afraid of something *associated with* flying.

Our brains haven't had a chance to evolve a fear of 'flying in planes', as they haven't really evolved much at all in all the time that we've had aeroplanes (which is only about 100 years, after all). What our brains and bodies can (and do) react to is being squashed into a tight space with thin air; seeing the ground sprawling out hundreds or thousands of feet below; accelerating suddenly to speeds of over 300 mph; feeling trapped and unable to stop, get off and escape; flying over a wide expanse of water; being in a wide, dark and unknowable sky, and so on. You can probably see how lots of small fears like these can easily add up to a big fear of the whole flight experience.

So getting over your fear of flying (if you have one) isn't really about understanding aeroplanes and flight procedures. It's about understanding what it is that's really

---

* Which, by my calculations, puts the odds of your plane crashing after being struck by an asteroid *and* a lightning bolt at the same time at roughly 1 in 160,000,000,000, 000,000 (160 quadrillion). Just in case you were wondering.

making you uncomfortable, and working on your emotional response to *that*.

In the meantime, you can rest (or at the very least, sit) safe in the knowledge that flying *really is* the safest way to travel. And you can make sure you stay extra safe and secure by doing the following every time you fly, just in case something should happen:

- Keep your seatbelt fastened whenever you're in your seat. But don't worry – this is less to do with preparing for a crash than it is avoiding getting bumped and bruised during unexpected air 'chop' or 'turbulence'.

- Make sure you study the plane safety card, so you know how to get out if you need to. Crashes and emergency landings are extremely rare, but if they do happen, you need to know how to get out quickly in case there's a fire, or the plane has to land on water.

- Listen to everything the flight attendants tell you, every time you fly, no matter how many times you think you've heard it. They're there to keep you and the other passengers safe, so if you ignore them, you're putting yourself and others at risk. Help them to do their job by listening and following instructions, and you'll be like an extra member of the safety crew!

Once you're prepared like this, you can feel happier and more in control. Then you can sit back, relax, and enjoy the whoosh and rumble of takeoff, the in-flight movies and games, the peculiar airline food and the whole flying experience.

COWBOY PILOT 'COMFORTS' FRIGHTENED PASSENGERS

Since I now have family in both the UK and the USA, I spend a lot of time flying back and forth across the Atlantic Ocean to see them. I don't mind flying so much, and I actually kind of enjoy the takeoff and landing bits, when the plane goes whooshing down the runway. But few people, I think, really enjoy it when the plane shakes and pitches around – a result of uneven airflow over the wings, known as *chop* or (if it's stronger) *turbulence*. Few people, it seems, except the pilot of one particular flight from Texas to London which I 'experienced' a few years ago.

Not long after takeoff, turbulence began to rock the cabin, and the seatbelt signs pinged on as the passengers jostled around in their seats. Having flown many times before, I knew that the 'Ping!' noise was usually followed by another 'Ping!' noise as the loudspeaker came on, followed by a comforting announcement from the captain or a flight attendant. something like:

'Ladies and gentlemen, please return to your seats. As you can see, the "fasten seatbelt" signs have been activated, so please ensure your seatbelts are properly secured, and return all tray-tables to an upright position. Just a little bit of choppy air, and we should be through it before too long. Nothing to worry about.'

Instead, this time, there was a 'Ping!' but no announcement, just breathing. Everyone looked up as the plane continued to pitch around. Eventually a message from the captain began.

'Ladies and gentlemen . . .' and then nothing.

Suddenly, the plane seemed to drop straight down out of the sky for a full two seconds, and almost everyone on the plane (me included) made an automatic, fearful, high-pitched 'Uunnnhhhhhh-hhhh!' sound.

'Woaaah!' cheered the captain over the loudspeaker, sounding like a cowboy atop a bucking horse.

The plane dropped again. For three seconds this time. A very long three seconds.

'Unnnnnnnnnnnnnnnhh-hhh!' went the passengers.

'Ha-haaaaa!!' chortled the captain, clearly insane.

Then the shaking and pitching seemed to soften, and eventually it stopped altogether. Were we safe? Was it over? All the passengers looked at each other with nervous smiles, awaiting an announcement from the captain to tell us what was going on.

'Ping!'

We all froze, listening.

'Ladies and gentlemen . . .' began the captain.

'Yes?' we all thought. 'What?'

'. . . you'd have to pay good money for a ride like that at Disneyland.'

The whole plane erupted in a ripple of groaning, nervous laughter. The sound was a mixture of giggling at the awful joke and pure relief that it was all, apparently, over.

I've flown many times since, but I've never experienced turbulence quite that bad again. Nor have I laughed quite as heartily as I did that day, thanks to the cowboy captain.

Disastrous derailment

At 10.56 am on 3 June 1998 a German Inter City Express (ICE) train was travelling at 125 miles per hour when it derailed and slammed into the pillars of a road bridge crossing over the tracks. The concrete bridge came crashing down on the train wreck and the many passengers inside. After the crash, rescue workers toiled for hours, sifting through twisted metal and amputated body parts in an effort to find survivors. In all, 101 people died and most of the 100 survivors were seriously injured. It was the worst train accident in Europe since 1945.

The fear

Ever stand on a platform as a big train whips through without stopping? That gives you some idea of the terrifying momentum that a speeding train has. A 100-tonne train weighs over 50 times as much as the average car. So in terms of momentum (mass multiplied by speed), being hit by a train travelling at 125mph is like being hit by a car travelling at over 6,000mph.*

Now imagine being inside a train like this as it hurtles out of control and derails. The terrifying screech of metal as your carriage folds up like an accordion and tumbles from the tracks. The sickening lurch as it rolls on to its side or roof, and the whole structure caves in . . .

The reality

The fear of trains (or *siderodromophobia*) isn't nearly as common as that of aeroplanes or boats. But it certainly does crop up, most often with people who have been in a *real* train accident at some earlier point in their lives.

---

* No car has ever done anywhere near 6,000mph, of course. The fastest jet aeroplanes can't even do half that speed. And the fastest car yet has only managed 750mph. But you get the idea.

However, it can also strike people who have no train-related upsets in their past at all, like those who were passengers in road (rather than rail) accidents. And this gives us a clue that something else might be happening with train-o-phobes.

Just as with the fear of aeroplanes, the fear of trains can have little to do with trains themselves at all. It may instead be a general fear of speed (*tachophobia*), of movement or motion (*kinetophobia*), or of being locked in (*cleithrophobia*). After all, all these things are part of the train-rider's experience. Trains move very fast, jerk to a start or halt, and wobble from side to side as they run. And many have doors that lock after departure.

Those things aside, riding a train is, in itself, definitely nothing to be afraid of. Travelling by rail is safer than travelling by air or sea, and it's far, far safer than travelling by road. The risk of being injured when travelling by train is at least twenty times less than when travelling by car. In fact, the total number of train passengers killed on British railways since they were first introduced over 170 years ago is less than the number of car passengers killed on British roads every year. And trains elsewhere in Europe, in Japan and in the USA are even safer.

The chances

The chances of being in a train crash vary across the globe, as more fatal crashes happen in developing countries compared with developed countries. But train safety is generally improving worldwide every year, and the odds of being caught in a fatal crash are still extremely low – between 1 in 60,000 and 1 in 140,000.

The lowdown

Trains are actually the safest way to travel quickly overland (or underground), and generally only a danger to us when we're in front of them rather than on them. While train passenger deaths are rare in the UK, every year over 200 people die after falling in front of trains, mucking about on train tracks, or stopping their cars at level crossings. So the lesson here is clear: getting on a train won't kill you, but getting on a train track will.

As with plane crashes and other rare transport accidents, train wrecks make for dramatic news. So when one happens somewhere in the world, it's usually all over the TV within the hour. Car accidents, on the other hand, are so common that they scarcely ever make the news (unless perhaps somebody famous is involved). Seeing this over and over again tricks us into thinking that train crashes are common and car crashes quite rare, when the truth is quite the opposite.

In fact, if all the drivers in Europe and North America who travel to work in cars every day switched to travelling by train (that's assuming they could, of course), it would save over 50,000 lives every year, or over 150 lives each day. How's that for a train of thought?

Fear Facts:

Because they're so heavy and fast, moving trains have enormous amounts of momentum and are very difficult to slow down quickly. When the driver on an average passenger train travelling at 55mph hits the brakes, it travels over a mile before stopping.

The fastest trains in the world are Magnetic Levitation (MagLev) trains, which use electrically powered magnets to hover (or levitate) above their tracks. With no friction between the wheels and tracks to slow them down, MagLev trains have been clocked at over 360 mph, otherwise known as 'pant-wetting speed'!

Tragedy strikes at sea

'"Mayday, Mayday. This is Estonia …" read the message, recorded by marine rescue authorities on the Finnish coast. The message broke off abruptly, suggesting a loss of power – perhaps water entering the machine room. It was the first and last contact with the ship. On board, severe vibrations woke passengers in their cabins. Many were unable to leave their rooms before all the lights went out. Eyewitnesses talked of panic and of people being left behind in the crush … There was little time to escape. Within a matter of minutes – not more than 30, according to some accounts – the ship had capsized and sunk, with the loss of more than 800 lives.'

The fear

Most of us have heard of the sinking of the *Titanic*, but that was almost a century ago, and there have been many other tragic accidents at sea in the years between. Like the *Herald of Free Enterprise*, a car-and-passenger ferry travelling from Belgium to England, which capsized just 2 miles out of port, drowning 193 people inside in March 1987. Or the *Estonia*, another ferry, which capsized en route from Estonia to Sweden, in which 852 people lost their lives in the icy waters of the Baltic Sea in September 1994. Or the *Princess of Stars*, capsized by a typhoon in the Philippines in June 2008, drowning over 800 passengers on board. All of these tragedies remind us of just how vulnerable we are when floating on the cruel, merciless ocean, and they all feed into *thalassophobia* – the fear of the sea.

The reality

It's true that whenever we put out to sea, we are vulnerable to the wind and waves. No ship is completely storm-proof, and even the largest cargo ships and oil tankers can be capsized or sunk by the worst kinds of weather. In fact, ships of this size (over 6,000 tonnes) are the riskiest to be on – you're roughly twice as likely to suffer drowning or serious injury on board one of these compared with smaller vessels. That's the bad news.

The good news is that boats designed to carry people (rather than cargo) are much safer, and passenger ferries are the safest ships of all. Ferries very, very rarely sink. The tragic losses of the *Estonia* and the *Herald of Free Enterprise* were not caused by a leaky hull or a faulty pump. They were the result of human mistakes. In both cases, people on board made mistakes that put the whole vessel at risk. The same was true of the *Titanic*. It wasn't really the monster iceberg that sank that ship, it was the captain.[*]

We've learned a lot from these past disasters, and used that knowledge to make ferries and other ships much safer. As a result, there have been no ferry passenger deaths in European waters since the *Estonia* disaster back in 1994. And while there have been others elsewhere in the world, ferries still rate as a pretty safe way to travel when compared to smaller vessels like yachts and speedboats.

As for these, there are a good number of small motor boat accidents each year, but very few are the result of faulty boats or boat equipment. Boating accidents are almost always caused by drivers or pilots who aren't paying attention, are driving carelessly, or are driving too fast. And of all the fatal accidents each year,

---

[*] . . . who decided to run the *Titanic* at top speed, in the dark, in an area known to have icebergs. Not so clever, perhaps.

an incredible 80–90% happen to people not wearing lifejackets. So the lesson is clear – boats are quite safe, as long as you handle them responsibly and wear the proper gear.

The chances

The odds of being in a fatal boating accident depend on how often you go boating, how experienced you are, and how you act while on board. When wearing a lifejacket while boating on a lake or close to shore, the odds of a fatal accident are very low. Speeding out to sea wearing nothing but a T-shirt . . . much higher. As for ferries, the odds differ depending on where you are in the world and what safety standards are like there, but in general ferry travel is very safe. In all, the odds of dying in a water transport accident are between 1 in 7,000 (for drowning) and 1 in 20,000 (for other kinds of on-board accident).

The lowdown

There will always be some risk involved in putting out to sea, as we can never perfectly predict the weather and sea conditions that often lead to accidents. But since most boating accidents are caused by people driving recklessly, colliding with other boats, or falling overboard without lifejackets, it's largely up to us how safe we stay when boating. As for ferries and larger ships, if you're on one of those, you're about as safe as you can get while at sea. And if wind and wave conditions get too 'choppy', the captain will most likely not put out to sea anyway. (Planes and trains generally won't leave airports or stations if bad weather makes the skies or rails too hazardous either. Ship, plane and train operators work by strict rules governing when they are and aren't allowed to set off in bad weather. So have a bit of trust in them too!)

As with the fear of planes and trains, the fear of being at sea is often more about the environment than the ship itself. You may have a more general fear of water or drowning, of the open space that surrounds you when you're on the open sea, or – if you suffer from sea-sickness – just the fear of vomiting (*emetophobia*). Figuring out which of these you suffer from would be the first step in working around a fear of being on board a boat, which usually means trying to get comfortable in shallow lakes or swimming pools first.

If you can't swim, learning to swim (or even to scuba dive)* with a patient instructor can be a great way to get more comfortable in the water. From there, you can try boarding boats while they're docked or on land, so that you can get used to being around them. Then by the time you take your first sailing trip you'll feel a lot more in control of your negative feelings – maybe not even feel them at all. Most of all, remember to take it all at your own speed, and your own pace. Do that, and it's all plain sailing.

---

* Seriously – there's nothing better for curing a fear of the sea than becoming a fish for a day!

The lane change he'll never forget

'I looked over my shoulder to see the other driver suddenly brake and swerve. From that moment it seemed as though everything was in slow motion. His car hit the rear of mine, sending me into a 180-degree spin. My car struck the metal barrier dividing the motorway, flipped over it, bounced upside down and rolled once more before coming to rest in the fast lane on the opposite side of the road. The sunroof had collapsed on to the back of my head, and I was bleeding heavily – struggling to retain consciousness.

By some miracle, an army convoy had been travelling in the opposite direction and managed to stop all oncoming traffic before my vehicle was hit again. They stayed with me until the helicopter arrived and airlifted me to hospital.'

Paul D., UK

The fear

Unlike most of the scary things we've looked at so far, car crashes are not rare events. They're extremely common, and unlike those you see in movies and TV series, people rarely walk away from a real car crash completely uninjured. When two cars collide head-on at 30mph, the effect is much the same as one car hitting a brick wall at 60mph. Your head snaps forward and back with a vicious whipping motion, causing injury to the brain, neck and spine. Your arms and legs can be smashed and crushed within the car's crumpling metal frame. And even if contact with a seatbelt or steering wheel stops you from flying through the windscreen, your heart can continue moving forward even after your chest is stopped, crushing it against your breastbone. At least 50 million people are seriously injured in car crashes every year. No wonder, then, that so many of the victims suffer from *amaxophobia* (or the fear of riding in a car) for years afterwards.

The reality

The simple truth is, on a list of 'safe ways to get around', cars are almost at the bottom.* This is partly because of the huge *number* of them on the roads – over 600 million of them at the last count – and because cars are just *used more* than other forms of transport. With that many cars swarming

---

* In fact, only motorbikes are worse. So maybe my mum was on to something when she told me I couldn't have one. Plus I was only 11 when I asked for it . . .

together on the world's roads, you would perhaps expect a good number of accidents and collisions.

But while the growing number of cars makes crashes more likely, the good news is that cars themselves are becoming safer to drive. Newer car models have sensors that can alert the driver if he drifts between lanes on a motorway, and brakes that can slow the car without skidding in an emergency. If a crash does happen, specially designed 'crumple' zones within the car's metal body scrunch up to absorb impact from the outside. Meanwhile, inside the car, rapidly inflating airbags cushion the passengers from being bashed against hard surfaces. And perhaps most importantly of all, seatbelts prevent the driver and passengers from being thrown against (or through) the windscreen.

Thanks to safety features like these, many crash victims' lives are saved at speeds under 50mph. Most crashes that result in deaths happen at speeds over 50mph, or where the passengers aren't wearing seatbelts (especially in the back seat). And this brings us to the main thing that affects how safe car travel really is – the driver.

In a few rare cases, the car causes the crash as its brakes, tyres or steering malfunction. But over 95% of crashes are due to drivers – driving too fast, too recklessly, or simply not paying close enough attention to the road and other cars. Poor or dangerous drivers fail to adjust their speed to suit the traffic and weather conditions (like a road made slippery by ice or pelting rain). They also drive too close to other cars, and make sudden turns and risky manoeuvres. Although these drivers *think* they're in control of the car, all of these things leave them unable to react if something goes wrong – like when the car in front suddenly brakes, or their tyres slip on the wet road.

Many people who think of themselves as 'good' drivers aren't altogether safe either. They can easily be distracted when they fiddle with radios, CD players, phones, food wrappers and drinks bottles while they drive. Even conversations with other passengers can be dangerously distracting. These drivers think they can do two things at once, but in reality the brain can only focus fully on one task at a time. So paying even a little attention to these 'other' things means they can't pay full attention to the road, and just as with the 'reckless' drivers, this leaves them unable to react in an emergency.

To stay safe on the roads we should all try to avoid these dangerous driving habits. For the driver, that means driving responsibly and safely, and not allowing yourself to be distracted. For the passengers, that means making sure you're not distracting the driver too much. So no more fighting over the armrest/ games console/ last bag of crisps, all right?*

---

* I mean it. I'll turn this thing around, and then *no one* gets to go to Chessington / Alton Towers / Disneyworld (delete as appropriate).

The chances

Car crashes are pretty common, and most people will experience at least one car accident within their lifetimes. The chances of being seriously injured or killed in a crash depend a little on where you live in the world (and how crowded the roads are), and a little on how old the driver is (drivers under 25 and over 75 are most at risk). But mostly it depends on how safe and careful the driver is. The odds range from 1 in 100 (for dangerous drivers on crowded roads) to 1 in 18,000 (for safe drivers on near-empty roads). For the average driver or passenger in Europe, Australia or the USA, the odds are probably around 1 in 1,500. Not terrible, but not too great either.

The lowdown

Travelling by car is such a common, everyday thing that we almost forget how dangerous it can be. It seems perfectly safe, but with so many cars on the road there's always the chance of an accident or crash. You're far more likely to be involved in an accident when travelling by car than you are when travelling by boat, train, plane or bicycle. In fact, over 97% of serious transport accidents involve cars rather than other methods of travel.

So it makes sense to stay safe when travelling by car, just in case. Most of us will never experience a serious, life-threatening car crash. But proper driving behaviour can help ensure we never do, and the proper use of car safety features can save our lives if the worst does happen. So whenever and wherever you're hitting the road, always make sure you do the following:

- Sit in the right place, and buckle up. Children under 12 are generally safer in the back seat, but sitting in the back is NO SAFER AT ALL IF YOU DON'T USE A SEATBELT. People often forget or neglect to use seatbelts in the back, as the seats in front give them a feeling of security. But in a real crash, you can fly right over the front seats and through the windscreen, maybe also injuring or killing the person in front of you.

- Sit up straight in your seat, rather than squirming around and letting the seatbelt slip off your shoulder or up over your stomach. Used correctly, a seatbelt will decrease your risk of dying in a serious crash by over 61%. Used incorrectly, it won't work as well, and could actually injure you.

- Don't dangle your arms or legs out of the window while the car is moving. In a serious crash, you might never see those bits again.

- Don't distract the driver by jumping about, making too much noise or doing anything to make them turn around in their seat to look at you.

- Take care as you get in or out of parked cars. Look for passing traffic before you open doors, and take special care as you get out of the car, always exiting on the pavement side if you can.

Fear Facts:

- Every year, around 1.2 million people are killed in car accidents, and at least 48 million more are injured worldwide.

- In the UK, almost 40,000 people are seriously injured or killed in road accidents every year. That's the same as a jumbo jet full of people every month.

- In the USA, someone dies in a car accident, on average, every 13 minutes.

The real killers

Over 1,000 children and young adults are killed on the world's roads every day.

Think about that for a minute – *a thousand, every day.* **That's an entire school full of people gone with every setting sun.**

Worldwide, no other thing kills so many young people between the ages of 10 and 24. No animal, no disease, no war and no other type of accident poses a larger threat to the survival of kids, teenagers and young adults than the common car. If horror movies reflected the real dangers in our lives, then the actors wouldn't be chased by ghosts, monsters, aliens and crazed murderers – they would be hit at random by murderous cars, driven by ordinary people.

The fear

Being struck by a car while on a bicycle or on foot is a genuinely terrifying experience. You could be thrown several metres in the air and land hard on the road with scrapes and broken bones. You could bounce up and over the front of the car that hits you, crashing against the glass windscreen and suffering terrible cuts and head injuries. Or worst of all, you could be dragged beneath the wheels of a car, van or lorry as its terrible weight grinds and crushes you beneath.

But interestingly, there is no name for the fear of 'being run over', as very few people actually have it. For all the dangers they pose to us, hardly anyone is actually *afraid* of cars, or of the perilous roads on which they speed past us. It's as if people are ignoring a herd of massive, fast-moving metal monsters that are constantly whipping around us – monsters which can injure or kill anyone unfortunate enough to stray before them. If you think about it, perhaps we *should* be afraid . . .

The reality

OK, so this one really is a serious danger. Road-traffic accidents are so common that many of us have been in them, seen them firsthand, or at the very least know somebody who has been in one. And they're never a pretty sight.

Tough as it is, the human body is no match for a speeding car. Even at 40mph, bones break and skulls shatter easily against the massive momentum generated by two tonnes of moving steel. Lucky traffic accident victims are bounced clear of the car and escape with minor injuries like broken wrists or ribs. The less lucky ones crack their heads when they fall, bounce into other objects, or slip under the wheels of the vehicle – all of which can prove fatal.

So should you be cowering away from road traffic, or happily strolling and cycling in among it? The answer is neither. You should always stay aware of just how dangerous road traffic can be, but if you take care when crossing roads and riding your bike, there's no reason why you can't safely and comfortably share the roads with cars, buses and lorries.

This is because cars and other vehicles very rarely mount kerbs or pavements to hit pedestrians, or suddenly swerve in the road to hit cyclists. It's usually the pedestrian or cyclist who causes the accident by entering the path of a car unexpectedly. This often happens for one of three reasons:

1) The car driver *doesn't expect you* to be in the road. This can happen when you cross the road at a corner or on the brow of a hill, or when you step out from behind a parked car or bus. To the driver, you seem to have appeared from nowhere, and they hit you before they can even react.

2) The driver *doesn't see you* in the road. This can happen when you're crossing the road or riding your bike at night, especially if you're wearing dark clothing.

3) The driver *sees you, but cannot stop in time.* This can happen if you cross the road away from pedestrian crossings and traffic islands, in 'fast' stretches of road where cars tend to pick up speed. The driver might see you and brake, but the fast-moving car may run or skid into you anyway.

If you can avoid putting yourself in any of these situations, then you're (almost) guaranteed to avoid getting into accidents on the road.

The chances

The odds of being fatally injured in a traffic accident vary across the world. They depend on how many cars there are on the roads, how safe the roads are to cross, and how well car drivers, cyclists and pedestrians stick to the laws and rules of the road. But in general the odds are fairly low, and a little better for cyclists (about 1 in 4,000) compared with pedestrians (about 1 in 500). Don't get too cocky if you're on a bike though – there are more pedestrians around than cyclists! Plus many cyclists wear protective helmets, while only the very strangest pedestrians do . . .

The lowdown

Nobody wants to be hit by a car, but plenty of people *are* hit, each and every day. Many of these accidents could easily be avoided. Some accidents are caused by reckless or bad drivers, but many (perhaps most) are the result of pedestrians and cyclists simply not taking enough care when using the roads. 'Taking proper care' means you need to:

- Cross the road at a safe place, like a pedestrian (zebra) crossing or traffic island. In particular, never cross at a bend in the road or near the brow of a hill, where approaching cars won't see you in time. Likewise, don't step out (or if on a bike, pull out) from between or behind parked cars or buses – you'll be hidden from view until the last minute, which is just asking for trouble.
- Make sure, wherever you cross, that you *stop, look both ways, and listen* for traffic before you cross the road. Listening is important because fast-moving cars can appear quickly, even after you've first checked the coast is clear. For the same reason, remember to *keep on looking and listening* as you cross.
- If you're on a bike or walking at the side of a road with no pavement, face the oncoming traffic and make sure you are easily visible. This means brightly coloured clothing during the day, and bright clothing AND lights at night.
- If you're riding a bike, wear a helmet (who cares if it looks a bit uncool? If you're hit, it could save your life) and make sure it's properly fitted and fastened.
- Learn the rules of the road, like the Highway Code for both cyclists and pedestrians. You can also take a

cycling proficiency test, which will make you a safer and better bike-rider.

Finally, remember this – as common as road accidents are, most kids make it through childhood (and most adults through their entire lives) without ever being knocked down or run over.

So treat the roads with the respect they deserve and you can make sure you're in the 'road-safe for life' group, rather than in the other, less fortunate one.

THE DAY I HIT A CAR

Growing up, almost every kid I knew rode a bicycle, and I had at least five friends who had been hit by cars while on them. My best friend Darren was hit by a van as he cycled around a roundabout. He was hit side-on, his leg was impaled on a piece of sharp, twisted metal sticking out of the front bumper, and he was dragged almost 50 feet along the road. Incredibly, he survived with a scar on his leg and little more.

My friend Sarah was in a child's seat on the back of her dad's bike when they were hit by a lorry. The lorry tipped over sideways as it swerved to avoid them, and fell on to them as it rolled right over. Her dad was thrown clear, but Sarah was stuck beneath the lorry in the twisted, tangled wreckage of the bike.

It took three firemen with cutting gear over an hour to get her out, but she escaped, amazingly, with just and few bumps and bruises and a scar on her hand.

As far as I know though, I was unique among my friends in being the only one to crash *into* a car rather than be hit *by* one.

I was on my bike, thundering down an alleyway that ran behind my house – a steep, downhill corridor between the neighbours' fences and back gardens on either side. The end of the steep valley opened out on to the pavement, kerb and road of a cul-de-sac at the bottom. I often raced down this alley on my bike, picking up speed, and jumping off the kerb at the bottom to land with a satisfying *thunk* on the (usually deserted) road.

This time, however, it wasn't deserted. At least not by the time I got to the bottom.

As I steadily picked up speed, the fences whooshing by on either side, I suddenly spotted a car pulling up to the kerb at the end of the alleyway. I tried the brakes, but they failed. Oops! Been meaning to fix those. Careering helplessly towards the side of the car, I tried to slow the bike by dragging my feet on the ground, but it was too late. WHAM! My bike stopped as it hit the side door of the car, while I kept going, over the top of it. I crash-landed face first in the road on the other side, carving wide, gravel-filled grazes into my right cheek and forehead.

The woman driving the car, at first alarmed by the thump and the sight of a wide-eyed kid flying over her roof, started shouting at me for denting her door. Thankfully, a neighbour (also my friend's dad, and a local doctor) saw the whole thing, rescued me from angry-car-lady, and spent the next hour patching me up before taking me home.

The graze eventually healed without a scar. But before it did, the single, huge scab running from my jaw to my hairline stuck around for weeks, looking like a giant crispbread stuck to my face. My brother – always a sensitive soul – called me 'Ryvita' right through that month.

Still – as car accidents go, I was luckier than most. It certainly made me more careful on my bike, and around cars, from that day on.

5 In the Bad Place

From Fears to Phobias

What's the difference between a fear and a phobia? Are they totally different, or basically the same thing? And where, exactly, do all these fears and phobias come from?

Well, we've already seen that fears come partly from the ancient history of our species (and the species that we descended from). Just like our eyes, ears, thumbs, lungs and brains, most of our basic fears evolved because they came in very handy for keeping us safe, and have helped our species to survive.

Eyes and ears, of course, helped our ancestors to hunt, to detect dangerous animals, and to know when a thunderstorm was coming. But it was fear that made them shrink back from the snakes, the lions and the lightning – fear that kept them alive in the presence of these and other dangers.

Fear is especially important to young animals (including

human babies and toddlers), because they're not really capable of looking after themselves. Or rather, they don't yet know enough about the world to keep themselves safe from harm. Very young babies aren't actually afraid of very much at all – or at least nowhere near as many things as older children are. Very few things make them cry out in fear (rather than in hunger, or in discomfort at a freshly filled nappy), but the two fears most common are: 1) being left alone, and 2) being handed to a strange, new person they're not familiar with. And if you think about it, that makes sense. A baby doesn't have to be afraid of much – it spends almost all of its time close (or even attached) to its mother, so is generally pretty well protected. The only thing a baby really has to fear is being abandoned, or being grabbed by someone who isn't one of its parents.

Young children, on the other hand, can toddle further from their parents, and have more chances to get themselves into trouble. If young children weren't at least *a little bit* afraid of the dark, high places, snakes, spiders and thunderclaps, then they would have a lot less chance of surviving to become teenagers and adults. Fears keep young children wary of the world's dangers while they figure out how everything works. Most things are considered 'dangerous, until proved safe'. Then, one by one, kids unlearn these fears as they grow up and learn to interact safely with the animals, people and environment around them.

Phobias, however, are a bit different from fears. Phobias

are fears which stretch out longer – or loom bigger in your mind – than they really should. Phobias make you more afraid of things than you should be, and left unchecked they can stop you from living a normal, happy life.

Most phobias are the result of a childhood fear that never went away. Sometimes this happens because the person had a really bad experience when they were little, like being bitten by a dog, or swallowing water and choking in a swimming pool. But more often, a fear becomes a long-lasting phobia because the person has never really *had* to get over it. Instead, they take steps to avoid the 'scary' thing at all costs. And while this does allow them to avoid feeling frightened and anxious, it also makes them *more* anxious about the 'scary' thing every time they do it. So when they finally do encounter a dog, an aeroplane, a swimming pool, or whatever it is they're afraid of, it seems *more* terrifying than ever before. The fear response is now way out of proportion to how scary the dog, plane or pool actually is. This is the main thing that separates fears from phobias.

In our prehistoric past, our ancestors had to hunt the world's forests and grasslands, and fish the world's seas and lakes to survive. But no hunter with a phobia of snakes in the grass would do very well on the hunt. And a fisherman with a phobia of being on the water would be lucky to catch anything at all. So just as fears can help very young children to survive, they can also do harm, by preventing us from doing the things we need to do as adults to live and thrive.

The problem is, unless they grow up in the wilderness

or countryside and still have to hunt or gather their own food, many children today can reach adulthood without ever learning to swim, to deal with snakes, or to cope with being alone and exposed in the dark. Most of the world's population now lives in cities and towns, where:

- no one is far from anyone else
- electricity provides light after dark
- people buy their fish, meats and vegetables, rather than braving the dark seas and forests to fish, hunt and gather food for themselves
- snakes and other wild animals are very rarely seen.

Little wonder, then, that far more phobias are seen in city dwellers rather than those who live off the land.

What do you do, then, if you've already got a phobia? Well, as usual, don't panic! There are ways to get around a phobia if you want to, or at the very least to become more comfortable with the idea of having one. So read on, and let's delve into the deepest, darkest depths of the mind, where fears lurk unseen inside us all . . .

Pitch-black panic

'I saw shadows everywhere, and imagined that stuffed toys and clothes flung over chairs were monsters and murderers lurking there in the semi-darkness. Worse yet, since I shared a room with my older brother, he would often go to bed after me and close the door fully. So I would manage to fall asleep in this half-light, but then wake up in the middle of the night, panicking in pitch darkness. This went on for quite a while, and for a long time I slept badly every night and woke up tired every morning – literally dragging myself out of bed and into school.'

The fear

What is it that makes being alone in the dark so terrifying? Simple – you've got no idea what could be lurking in it! Imagine this:

Feeling your way through the lightless depths of a cave, your hands stretched out before you, your fingers suddenly fall upon a mass of writhing worms or scuttling spiders . . .

Camping in a forest on a moonless night, you hear a rustle of leaves and a cracking twig outside your tent. Breathing hard, you poke your head outside to investigate, but you see only pitch blackness . . . and the sounds are getting louder and closer . . .

Waking in your bed in the middle of the night, you suddenly feel a presence in the room. Is it a creeping burglar? A freakish monster? An evil spirit? You're desperate to know, but to switch on the light you'd have to cross the room, to make a noise . . . and then *it* would know you were there . . .

The reality

Nyctophobia, or fear of the dark, is extremely common in children, and surprisingly common in adults too. Like many phobias, it comes from a fear we're born with – a healthy fear which can help us to avoid danger and harm.

We humans, like most mammals, are very visual creatures. We depend on our eyesight for all kinds of things, like spotting food, recognizing faces, judging distances, catching, throwing, aiming, dodging, fighting and more.

Robbed of our sense of sight, most of us tend to . . . well, freak out a bit. We find it hard to relax, hard to keep our balance, and hard not to jump at the slightest sound or touch. If you want to test this out, try closing your eyes and *slowly* walking around the room. You'll probably find that your breathing will get faster, you'll flinch at every object you brush past or bump into, and you'll desperately want to cheat and open your eyes throughout the experiment. Not easy to do calmly, is it?

In one way, this makes perfect sense. No one likes bumping into or tripping over things. So a healthy fear of being cast into darkness will slow you down, make you more alert, and make you move carefully enough to avoid objects and pitfalls. To our ancestors living on the plains and savannahs of Africa, this fear was obviously very important for survival. If they weren't so wary of the dark, then a lot more of them would have ended up accidentally strolling into rivers and ravines, or straight into lions, rhinos and people from unfriendly tribes. What's more, this instinct still protects us today – even those of us who don't live with wild animals and terrain. If we're outside in a town or city at night, we don't want to wander down dark alleyways or dawdle into dangerous building sites either.

The problem is that this instinctive, 'healthy' fear of the dark and real *nytcophobia* are two different things. It's one thing to be alert in darkened places and quite another thing to have a paralysing terror of the darkness itself. People with a real phobia of the dark can't sleep without the lights on, panic when the lights go off, and can't enter a darkened room without a thumping heartbeat and a churning stomach. Once a fear turns into a phobia like this, it can stop someone from living a happy life, as they feel trapped by their fears – trapped by the need to see what's around them at all times. That may be fine while you have the choice of keeping the lights on every night, everywhere you go, but what if there's a power cut? How sad, too, that you'll miss out on things like star-gazing and camping out, far from where the glow from houses and street lights can comfort you.

The good news is that it's possible to get over or around fears and phobias, and the fear of the dark is probably one of the easier ones to handle. All you have to do is retrain your brain, and help it to realize that the darkness itself isn't harmful. Sure, the darkness can hide things that *could* harm you – things like cliff edges, startled bears and shifty people. But you also find these things only in certain places. So all you have to do to stay safe in the dark is avoid walking near cliffs, through unknown wilderness and down shifty streets by night. Alone in your house, the only things in the dark that can hurt you are furniture, toys, electric cables and other objects you might blunder into. And pretty much the worst that could happen to you is a bump, a bruise or a stubbed toe. Once you realize that 'the dark can't hurt you', it's just a case of getting used to the dark, by immersing yourself in it little by little until you become comfortable.

The chances

Since the dark itself is not dangerous, it can't really hurt you at all. It is possible, of course, to trip over or fall and *hurt yourself* in the dark, so you should take care moving around in it – especially if you're in an unfamiliar place. But even if that does happen, it's the *object* or the *fall* that does you damage, not the dark itself. So while your chances of hurting yourself *in* the dark are higher than in fully lit places, your chances of being hurt or harmed *by* the dark are exactly zero!

The lowdown

Fear of the dark, like most other phobias, is mostly about feeling panicked and out of control. You don't know what's in the dark, and you feel that the only way of regaining control is to switch the lights on to check. But if you really think about it, what kinds of things are really likely to be lurking in the dark, waiting to get you? Ghosts? Monsters? Aliens? As we'll see in the next chapter, you have nothing to fear from them. Wild animals? Creepy people? Maybe you would (and should) be worried about those if you were out in the wilderness or on city streets by night, but if you're locked up safe within your own home, then it's very unlikely that anyone or anything could've crept in while you slept.*

So rather than having to switch the lights on, or keep them on all the time, there's another way to

---

* Unless you have a ninja or a wild animal already living in your house . . . in which case, frankly, you're asking for trouble.

regain the feeling of control in the dark. You just try to get used to it bit by bit, by gradually making yourself more comfortable with the idea of being in the dark. Psychologists call this 'acclimation therapy' or 'graded exposure', and it works really well for most people who try it.

If you want to try this, all you have to do is put yourself in a room in semi-darkness – as dark as you feel comfortable with, but no more. Then, close the door a little to cut some light from outside (or use a dimmer switch to dim the light in the room). Now you've made it a little darker, you just sit and breathe normally until you feel comfortable. If you feel your breathing speed up, try to slow it down by breathing more deeply on purpose. If that doesn't work, put the lights back up a bit until you do feel better, and then try again after a few minutes. Eventually you should be able to extinguish most or all of the light in the room without feeling panicked or nervous. You can take as long as you like to do this – a few days, a few weeks, a month – but most people find the process much easier, and much faster, than they expect.

By getting control of your breathing like this, you can stop the build-up of panic before it begins, and eventually you'll be able to feel in control of your fears and emotions without having to switch the light on to take a peek. You'll be free of your phobia, and you can join the owls, the cats, the moths and the bats in your fearless friendship with the night!

ONE FEAR CONQUERS ANOTHER

As I described on page 179, I was scared of going to sleep in the dark right up until I was about 10 years old. When I was little, that meant my parents had to leave a small lamp or night-light on when putting me to bed. After a while, though, they began turning the lights off at night to try and get me out of the habit. This worked . . . up to a point. The thing was, I could handle having the room lights off, but I still wasn't comfortable with complete darkness. To avoid panic, I still had to have the hall light on and the bedroom door open a bit, to let some light spill in.

Even in my low-lit room I was terrified. Worse yet, my older brother would often go to bed after me and close the door fully. So I would wake up in the middle of the night, panicking in pitch darkness. This went on for quite a while, and for a long time I slept badly every night and woke up tired every morning – literally dragging myself out of bed and into school.

In the end, it was the fear of something else – embarrassment – that got me over my fear of the dark. When I stayed over at friends' houses, I was embarrassed to keep on asking that they 'leave the door open a crack' at bedtime, and one friend in particular took great delight in making fun of my 'big baby' fear of the dark. So one night I decided to get rid of it – not get over it, just get rid of it, once and for all. And I did.

I went to bed early, switched off the lights, and slowly closed the door. Once in bed, I went through all the same things as usual – jumping at every creaky floorboard and every yowling cat outside. But since I couldn't see anything at all, I couldn't imagine that the crumpled school tie on the floor was an oversized mutant tarantula, or that the dressing-gown on the door was actually a hooded madman waiting to strike. So my imagination eventually dried up and gave in, and I drifted off to sleep. I slept soundly that night, and woke up feeling rested and proud that I'd managed to conquer my fears after so long. From that day on, I slept in the dark every night.

But, unfortunately, I also needed a new excuse for not wanting to get up for school in the mornings . . .

Water and Drowning

That sinking feeling

'Scratching desperately at the tiled side of the pool, I watched tranquil shafts of sunlight waver in the water. I tried to cram my stubby fingertips into the grout of the pool's tiles, trying – and failing – to find some sort of handhold. Alone and sinking downward, a shrill series of screams left my young mouth – but they were lost as soon as they were uttered, transformed into mute bubbles. An eternity later, the heavy water darkened around me. My limbs grew weary from frantic windmilling; my lungs ached; my eyes closed, surrendering. As I choked and sputtered with the sting of chlorine, a hand reached down into the shadowy depths and yanked me upward to the bright air. Gasping and shivering, I realized my saviour had been not my mother – who was sitting off to the side of the pool, reading – but the pool's owner.'

The fear

For many people, drowning is their worst nightmare. In fact, along with being chased and falling, drowning is one of the most common nightmares there is. It's pretty easy to see why. The helpless panic as water fills your mouth, your nose, your throat and your lungs. The burning pressure in your chest as you try to hold in what little air you have left, hoping against hope that you'll reach the surface in time. Your limbs growing heavier and harder to move. Your body, weighed down with water, sinking further and further from the world above. And the terrible, silent slip into unconsciousness . . .

The reality

Unlike other phobias – like those of animals, needles and open spaces – the fear of water and drowning (or *aquaphobia*) turns up in every country and culture, and it is one of the top three most common phobias worldwide.

On some level, everybody fears drowning. If you think you don't, all it will take is one near-drowning experience to show you that you really do. Like the fear of the dark, it's programmed into your brain and nervous system as a healthy warning against putting yourself in mortal danger. But comparing the two, your body's response to drowning is far, far more powerful than its response to finding itself in the dark.

This is because, quite simply, the danger of drowning is so much greater than that of being attacked or injured in the dark. If you're lucky, you can survive in the dark for days, months, or years. But you can't survive for more than a few minutes with your lungs full of water.

To continue living, your brain and body need a constant supply of oxygen. Of course, they need nutrients (or food) and water too, but since your body can store nutrients and water in cells and tissues, it can go days or weeks without those. Oxygen, on the other hand, can't be stored long-term in your body. It gets shifted around and used up very soon after entering your bloodstream, which is why you have to keep breathing – in, out, in, out – non-stop, 24 hours a day, just to stay alive.* Luckily, your body does this automatically and unconsciously – without your having to think about it. Otherwise it'd be tough getting anything else done!

With each breath in, oxygen moves from the air in your lungs into your blood, and from there it gets carried throughout your body by special proteins called *haemoglobins*. Once in the cells and tissues, oxygen is used (along with water and carbon-based molecules from food) to create energy. That energy powers every organ and system in your body, including your brain, heart, lungs,

---

* At an average rate of 15 breaths per minute, the average number of breaths we take in an entire lifetime is roughly 400 million. And since we breathe in, on average, about half a litre of air per breath, that means we breathe about 200 million litres of air in a lifetime. That's enough to fill over 300 hot-air balloons! I wouldn't want to try it though. Air-beds and armbands are fine, but trying to inflate an aircraft by yourself is just silly . . .

kidneys, intestines and more. In turn, these control your thoughts, your movements, your digestion and pretty much everything else that keeps you ticking.

Denied oxygen for even a minute, your body quickly burns through its reserves of oxygen from previous breaths, and carbon dioxide builds up in the brain, bloodstream and lungs. Sensing this, the brain begins to shut parts of itself down (causing you to pass out) as it tries to conserve what little energy-giving oxygen is left. In open air, this often isn't so bad. You may pass out, but there's a good chance you'll recover, provided your air supply is replaced and your breathing restarts. Underwater, the first breath after passing out fills the depths of your lungs with water, stopping any more air getting through to the bloodstream – even if your unconscious body floats up (or is pulled up by a rescuer) to meet fresh air at the surface.

Knowing this, your body's response to finding itself underwater and without air is a powerful one. Once the low-oxygen, high-carbon-dioxide state is detected, the brain's ancient 'fight-or-flight' system kicks in almost immediately, speeding your heartbeat and redirecting more blood to the muscles to help you struggle your way to the surface for more air. Once there, your lungs pull in deep gasping breaths to replace the lost oxygen quickly and return your body to normal.

This is all fine as far as it goes. But the problem is that for an *aquaphobic*, this system gets triggered early. If you have a true phobia of water, even the thought of putting your head underwater (or of being over water, on a boat or bridge) can trigger the powerful 'fight-or-flight' response. So the person begins to react as if they're drowning – with gasping breaths, flailing limbs and a pounding heart – when they haven't so much as dipped a toe in the water.

Happily, though, death by drowning is actually a pretty rare occurrence, and, provided you're careful in the water, it's unlikely to happen to you. As long as you avoid being caught in a current, caught out of your depth, trapped beneath the surface, or knocked unconscious while in the water, you need never get to the point where you experience the panic of drowning at all. Even for those who do, many are rescued and revived by quick-acting lifeguards and bystanders. Stay smart, and you can enjoy the water in safety. And as with other phobias, even the all-powerful *aquaphobia* can be overcome.

The chances

Your odds of drowning depend a little on how strong a swimmer you are, but also on where you find yourself submerged. The odds of drowning in a swimming pool are only about 1 in 7,000, but the odds of drowning in natural water bodies (lakes, seas and rivers) are more than double that, at around 1 in 3,000.

The lowdown

As with other instinctive, 'primal' fears, the fear of water is an understandable one if you take into account how easily and quickly a body of water can do us in! But if you learn to swim, you understand the dangers, and you have a healthy respect for the water, there's no reason why you can't learn to enjoy travelling, playing and living with water without panic or dread.

For aquaphobics, learning to swim (or even scuba dive) with a patient, sensitive instructor can be a great way to conquer your fear of water, as long as you take it very slowly, and at your own pace. But if you don't want to go that far, you can at least learn to be more comfortable around the water through acclimation therapy, similar to that used for other phobias.

For everyone who loves (or learns to love) the water, it's still worth bearing in mind that being in and around water can be dangerous if you're not careful and smart about it. For swimming pools, this means:

- no swimming alone or unsupervised – so there's always someone to help if something goes wrong
- no running – so that you don't slip, whack your head, and fall in while unconscious
- no diving in shallow water, as hitting your head on the bottom is a pretty bad idea too.

That said, swimming pools are still safer than open water sources like lakes, rivers and seas. This is partly because they tend to be smaller, shallower and more closely watched – so if you do get into trouble, it's easier to struggle out and more likely that someone will spot you and come to your aid. But it's mostly because natural waters are more varied and unpredictable than artificial pools. They may be freezing cold and cause shock and hypothermia. They may hide rocks, discarded fishing nets and other underwater dangers. And unlike pools, they may have powerful currents and waves. River and coastal sea currents can drag you under, or pull you far from the shore, and a big wave can bash you against rocks or hard against the sea bed.

So stay safe by the seaside and lakeside by doing this:

- Find out about the water before you plunge in. Is it a known safe spot for swimming? If not, best not to risk it – find somewhere else.
- If it's too rough or choppy, give it a miss. Big waves can be fun, but if they're big enough to toss you into things, it's probably not worth it.
- In the water, take notice of boats, jet skis, surfboards and anything else that might be whipping about nearby. There are often marker buoys to tell you where the boating areas for these begin, so don't stray beyond those and you'll be safer.

And finally,

- Beware of strong currents. It's all too easy for a current to whisk you further out than you wanted to go before you notice. So keep a close eye on the shore, and you won't find yourself halfway to Greenland on your inflatable air-bed.

Fear Facts:

- Children under 5 and young people aged 15–24 have the highest drowning rates, and about 20% of drownings involving children happen in public swimming pools, with lifeguards present.

- It's possible to drown in just 5cm of water, so people drown not only in seas and swimming pools, but also baths, buckets and paddling pools.

Dizzy heights

'I happen to have a really bad fear of heights. Trust me – it's no fun at all. When you look down from high up, it feels like you're going to faint, and you just want to get down. If you lean over something and look down, you feel really scared, you go all tingly, and your body automatically pulls you back from the edge. The worst thing is how embarrassing it is. Here are some of my 'greatest hits' so far:

1) On our school trip, we had to go up a really high ladder to go abseiling. I was the only one who didn't get up. I got to the 10th step (a new record for me!), but then I had to climb down.

2) When we later went to a ski slope, I was the only one that couldn't get to the top. So I had to ski down from only halfway . . .

3) I was on a trampoline once (one where you can go really high, wearing a harness around your waist), and I jumped up and . . . wet myself. What a horrible moment!'

Jake M., Wales

The fear

Imagine slipping and tumbling from the roof of a skyscraper, or being sucked out of a speeding aeroplane,* to find nothing but a few thousand feet of cold air between you and the ground. The air roars past your ears. Your clothes flap and snap against your body as you tumble dizzily in the wind. You stare wide-eyed at the Earth far beneath you, as the terrible pull of gravity draws you ever closer towards becoming a crumpled mess (or perhaps just a messy stain) on the ground. Your limbs flail and flap wildly in a hopeless effort to slow your fall. But you are no dainty bird on the wing. You are a big, heavy person. And fall you will . . .

The reality

OK, the fact of the matter is, we humans can't fly. At least not without aeroplanes or hang-gliders.

We're also quite squishy and brittle as animals go, so if dropped from a great height on to a hard surface, even the toughest bits of our bodies will shatter like glass (while the squishiest bits burst like balloons).

Put these two facts together, and you see that we have every reason to fear falling from high places, and every reason to avoid being in high places if we possibly can. Put most people on the roof of a 50-storey skyscraper and tell

---

* I often think about this when using aeroplane toilets. Although I know it's pretty much impossible, I have visions of myself being sucked down the pan and out of the aeroplane along with the loud WHOOSH! of the vacuum flush. This never happens, of course. Come to think of it, if it did happen, my bum would probably plug the small drain hole shut anyway . . .

them to stand on the edge and peer down, and you'll see wide eyes, a sharp intake of breath, and a quick retreat back to a safe distance.

But for an *acrophobic* (someone with an extreme fear of heights), the same reaction might kick in at just 50 centimetres off the ground rather than 50 storeys. What's more, an *acrophobia* sufferer might also experience vertigo – a dizzying sensation of lost balance which makes them teeter and wobble like a newborn deer calf as they try to get their balance back. Worse still, vertigo doesn't always need a height to happen. It can also be felt by *agoraphobics* (people who have panic attacks in wide open spaces, shopping malls, supermarkets, or even their own homes) who are firmly at ground level.

So what's going on here? Well, just as with most other phobias, *acrophobia* and *agoraphobia*[*] begin with simple fears that serve a useful purpose, but later grow into uncontrollable states of dread and panic.

A healthy fear of heights, of course, teaches you to beware the obvious dangers of falling from cliffs, trees, buildings and other high spots. Everybody, to some extent, is born with this. People who seem fearless of heights – like circus acrobats, Hollywood stunt men and construction

---

[*] As these sound so similar, people often mix and combine them when talking about them. But not all agoraphobics are also 'acros', and not all acrophobics are 'agoros', either. Confusingly, there's also another one called *acarophobia*, which is the fear of itching. So I guess an *agoro-acro-acarophobic* would be someone who has nightmares about being in a high-up open space wearing that scratchy all-wool jumper their auntie bought them for Christmas.

workers who stride between roof beams and scaffolds – have generally un-learned this natural fear of heights by being exposed to heights every day for months or years.

Likewise, many animals (some more than others) fear being caught out in the open, or in places they feel they're unable to escape from, because they know they have nowhere to hide if attacked by a predator. Humans are no exception to this, which is one reason why most of us feel more comfortable surrounded by trees or buildings than we do when surrounded by featureless moors, deserts or plains. In these 'wide open' spaces, even though you can see everything for miles around, you feel exposed and vulnerable – because deep down you know you have nowhere to run or hide.

So some acrophobics and agoraphobics simply have more intense (and more easily triggered) versions of fears we all share. They just have stronger emotional responses to heights and places that most of us don't think of as *that* high, *that* open, or *that* dangerous.

But what about the dizziness, wobbling and falling over? Surely, that's just about the worst thing you could do if you found yourself looking over a high ledge or cliff, right? And how does toppling over help if you find yourself exposed and at risk of attack?

Well, these things don't help. At all. Unlike our basic fear responses, dizziness and wobbling aren't of any use to us in dealing with heights or open spaces. They're the result of a malfunctioning system within the body – one that your brain uses to sense which way up you are, and to keep you on balance.

To keep your body balanced, your brain collects and combines three types of information from the body and your surroundings. The first comes from the muscles, which contain tiny gauges or receptors that detect how stretched out or compressed each muscle is. Putting the signals from these receptors together, the brain can map out where each bit of the body is in relation to all the others. This is called *proprioception*, and it's how you know where your arms, legs, fingers and toes are even with your eyes closed.

The second type of information comes from the eyes. The eyes take in objects and features of the landscape around you, and the brain uses these as cues to tell, say, which way up you are, and how far you are from the ground and other objects.

The third and final type of information comes from the inner ears, where special fluid-filled organs (called the vestibular organs) sense the pull of gravity, helping you to know which way is up (or rather, down) without having to look or think.

In most healthy people, the brain puts all these bits of evidence together to build a complete picture of where the body is in Space, keeping them upright and on balance. But if you have damaged or altered vestibular organs, then the information from the eyes and ears doesn't always seem to match up, which can confuse the brain and make you feel like you're leaning or toppling over when you're actually standing up straight.

This happens especially when your eyes have trouble judging the distance to the ground – such as when you're very high up. This may explain why many acrophobics seem to lose their balance when they find themselves up high. But it can also happen when your eyes have trouble judging the distance to the nearest object to you – such as when you're in a wide open, featureless space . . . or in the middle of a cavernous shopping mall, far from the walls and high ceilings. This, in turn, could explain why many agoraphobics topple over in wide open spaces, and feel like they have to cling to walls before they stop feeling dizzy.

The chances

The odds of being hurt or harmed *by* (rather than in) an open space, shopping mall or supermarket are zero. Meanwhile, the average odds of a fatal fall in the USA* look something like this:

---

* Not that the USA is a particularly dangerous place. Once again, it's just where the best records and figures for these sorts of things are kept. So that people can sue each other. Often within seconds of falling.

from a ladder or scaffolding	1 in 9,000
from a tall building	1 in 6,500
from a chair or bed	1 in 5,800
down stairs or steps	1 in 2,500

The lowdown

Like other phobias, *acrophobia* and *agoraphobia* can be just extensions of natural fears, or fears left unchecked and running out of control. For people who have full-on panic attacks at heights or in open spaces, acclimation therapy can help them get their fears under control. This could mean taking them to tame heights and spaces and progressing to bigger ones, or it could even mean using Virtual Reality (VR) programs to get them used to the sensations of being up high / outside before they try it for real. (Phobics with inner-ear problems, though, may also need medicines or special treatment to help relieve their dizziness.)

Ultimately, the good news is that the spaces and heights feared by agoraphobics and acrophobics really aren't, for the most part, very dangerous at all. In the modern world (rather than the more ancient world of hunters and gatherers), most people have little to fear from being 'caught in the open' any more. And they certainly don't have to worry about being attacked by wild animals in shopping malls and supermarkets. (Well, not the ones I go to, anyway.) So the chances of being harmed or killed in an open space are extremely low. Or at least no worse than anywhere else.

As for heights, it's good, of course, to avoid clambering and skipping about at dangerous heights without climbing ropes and harnesses. Unless of course you're a trained rock climber, a ninja* or one of those free-running Parkour guys that do somersaults off buildings.

Beyond that, just remember that far more tragic plummets and falls happen on household stairs than they do from cliffs, trees and tall buildings. So the moral of the story is – be careful on the clifftops, but take *real* care on the stairs!

EXTREME HEIGHTS THERAPY

Despite my successful conquering of 'The Dark', my childhood fear of heights lingered on until I was about 16. It wasn't just really high buildings and cliffs either. Basically, being any higher than 2m up (and especially being near sheer drop-offs or edges) would make me feel as if my brain was dropping into my knees. When my friends and I climbed trees I'd do it with them, but I hated every minute of it – feeling dizzy and like I needed to pee throughout the whole experience. When the class went to visit the famous White Cliffs of Dover, near the town where I grew up, I stayed waaaaay back from the cliff edge while the others enjoyed the views of the port, the

---

* And even they have to be careful, or risk doing themselves a ninja-ry. Ha-haa!

beaches, and the English Channel below. But unlike being in the dark, I could usually avoid being in high places if I wanted to, so there wasn't such a need to get over this particular fear. So on it went – well into my teens.

Then one day my friend Neil returned from one of those 'adventure holidays' in Wales, where he had learned to rock climb, abseil and more. He was keen to start climbing back in Kent (where we lived), and wanted a partner to go with him. He had all the gear – rope, harnesses, shoes, everything – and was happy to teach me how to use it. I thought about it, and decided maybe it was a good chance to see if I could conquer my fear of heights. I figured I'd either become a fearless spider-man, or resign myself to avoiding high places for life.

So off we went to a local woods, where an old, disused railway bridge was used by Scout groups to practise climbing and abseiling. It was a red-brick arch bridge about 30m tall, which spanned a stream valley in the forest.

'We start at the top,' said Neil, suiting up in the climbing harness, and tying ropes to trees and himself. 'We'll abseil down, then climb back up. That way, it'll be scary at first, but you'll get lower to the ground with every step, and you'll crack your fear of heights before you try to scale it.'

That seemed to make sense. 'OK – what do I do?' I replied.

'Just watch me first' said Neil, looping a pair of ropes into a steel ring on his belt. 'OK – *this* is your descending line, and it goes through *here* and you hold it like *this* . . . you hold on to this one, no matter what, OK?'

'What happens if I don't?' I whimpered back. 'Will I fall?'

'Naaaah,' said Neil, grinning, 'that's what this other one is for.' He grabbed the other rope, and whipped it up and down, sending ripples to the other end, which was fastened to a nearby tree. 'This is your safety line. Even if you let go of the first one, this one will stop you falling. Look – watch this . . .'

And with that, he stepped backwards to the edge of the bridge, the hard forest floor yawning away 30 metres beneath him. He began to lean back over the edge, putting his weight on the ropes without holding on with his hands. 'See? Safe as houses. It's – wooooaaaaaaaaaaaaaaaaaaaaaaaa!' . . . at which point he promptly fell off the edge.

Luckily, though, he'd managed to scrabble a one-handed grip on to the stone edge itself, and I ran forward to grab his arm and help pull him back up.

'Sorry – wrong rope,' he said breathlessly. 'Let's try that again.'

As you might imagine, I wasn't exactly filled with confidence in Neil as a climbing teacher after that. But, incredibly, we did abseil and climb the bridge that day, three times each. And via Neil's unusual brand of 'extreme fear therapy', I lost my fear of heights that very day!

Boxed in and up high? No way!

'When I was younger, it was my dad who was afraid of things, especially of going into small tight spaces. I guess he started being claustrophobic when he was a kid, but he is still as an adult. My family went on vacation to St Louis, where the most famous monument is the St Louis Arch. It is the tallest national monument in the USA at 630 feet (192m). To get to the top, you have to ride in a tiny, box-like tram car that seats only 5 people. It takes 4 minutes to get to the top. When it came time for us to get on the tram, my dad got scared and pointed at my brother, who was only 4 at the time, and said, "We just can't go on – Brian will be too scared." Sure, blame it on the 4-year-old!'

Heather M., USA

The fear

Ahh – *claustrophobia*. The fear of being trapped in tight or enclosed spaces. Not everyone freaks out at the thought of being trapped in the cold, metal confines of an unmoving lift. But practically everyone shivers at the thought of being buried alive, or stuck fast in a dark, damp tunnel, deep under the ground. If that doesn't bother you, how about being crushed within a thick crowd of panicking people, or knocked to the ground and trampled by an angry mob of hundreds or thousands?

If thinking about that makes you tense, then like most people in the world you don't much fancy the idea of being squashed or suffocated. But if it makes your chest feel tight, your breathing quicken, your shoulders hunch, and your neck shrink inward like a startled tortoise . . . then you are among the world's many true *claustrophobes*.* And you can probably imagine no worse a fate than being trapped and crushed to death.

The reality

Tight spaces can be dangerous places, and your brain and body know it. So as with heights, wide open spaces and the dark, the origins of this fear come from a nervous alarm system that evolved in our animal ancestors, helpfully reminding them (and now us) to stay safe.

Understandably, we all show some wariness of being in situations or places where we might be crushed or suffocated. Our bony skulls and ribcages typically do a fine job of keeping the delicate organs inside from being

---

* *-phobes* and *-phobics* are two different ways of describing people with phobia conditions. The opposite is *-philes*, as in *aquaphiles* (people who like being in the water), *aerophiles* (people who like flying) and *arachnophiles* (people who just luurve spiders). As my mum always says, 'It takes all sorts.'

squashed and punctured. But pile enough stuff (or people) on top of us, and our bony crash-helmets and chest-guards will eventually crack and give way, fatally damaging the brain, lungs and other organs inside. And we've already seen how little time we can last without breathing, so fear of tight, airless spaces is understandable too. In short: breathing and keeping your proper shape – good; *not* breathing, or being flattened like a pancake – bad. *Very* bad.

But while *claustrophobia* is partly about feeling crushed or suffocated, it's mostly about feeling trapped and unable to escape. This, of course, is understandable too. After all, our animal ancestors didn't want to find themselves trapped and unable to run from predators any more than they wanted to be squashed or suffocated. But very often, serious *claustrophobes* and *melanophobes* (people who fear crowds specifically) still have quite a bit of space and breathing room around them when they begin to panic. The walls or crowds aren't closing in – they're just, well, *there*. And that alone is enough to trigger the *feeling* of being crushed and suffocated.

As with other phobias, the body's physical 'danger'

responses kick in before any real danger is present, causing quickened breathing and tense muscles (especially in the chest, as the rapid panting soon tires the muscles of the ribcage and diaphragm, which lie around and beneath the lungs). But for claustrophobes, these sensations can feel particularly nasty, as their worst fears seem to be coming true. They fear feeling crushed and breathless, and yet the body's own response to that fear leaves them feeling as if their chests are being crushed and their lungs are unable to take in enough air. This will often kick off a cycle of panic and overly rapid breathing (or *hyperventilation*) that only ends when the claustrophobe escapes the room, space or crowd* and feels like they're able to move and breathe freely again.

In reality, however, very, very few people meet with injury or doom when trapped in crowds, tunnels or rogue lifts. And claustrophobia, if left unchecked, can worsen to the point where you can't bear to enter even normal-sized rooms and houses, or face even the smallest crowds of people on the street. So if you have it, the best thing you can do is try to understand it, to realize that most tight spaces and crowds are *not*, in fact, dangerous, and to work with a therapist or psychologist until you can get around the 'can't escape!' feeling.

---

* Either that or they pass out – which isn't too great in the middle of a rock concert or football crowd either. At worst, you'll be trampled and danced on by people who fail to spot you. At best, you'll wake up covered in sticky soft-drink residue and bits of half-eaten meat pie.

The chances

The odds of being hurt in a tight space vary depending on what kind of space it is, and how far you are from help if you do in fact become trapped. Cupboards and wardrobes, for example, hardly ever suffocate people. So even if, say, an evil younger brother traps you inside one, don't panic – you'll be out again, unharmed, soon enough. This is because cupboards and wardrobes are never completely airtight, and are typically found inside houses, so someone (usually an angry parent) will find you before too long. (And then – hahaaa! – your little brother is *in for it*!)

Likewise, lifts, even malfunctioning ones, aren't particularly dangerous places to be. Most lifts aren't airtight either, so you're unlikely to run out of air even if you're stuck in there for hours, or even days. In the UK and US, fewer than 10 people a year die in accidents related to lifts, and this almost always involves someone stepping into an empty lift shaft* rather than being stuck inside the lift.

Being crushed in crowds and trapped in rail or road tunnels is also rare, so they're nothing much to worry about either. The only real risks in tight spaces come with being trapped underground, which can happen if you go caving or potholing without proper gear and training, or if you're daft enough to try 'exploring' disused mines, tunnels, caves and building sites by yourself. Every few weeks, some poor

---

* An important safety tip, that – always check the lift is *actually there* before getting on it. Being very clever, I usually do this with horses, trains, buses and aeroplanes too . . .

kid somewhere dies as a dangerous underground tunnel or construction trench collapses on them. So if the sign says KEEP OUT, take notice – it's there for a reason.

In all, your odds of being in a fatal cave-in or accidental burial are about 75,000 to 1, and your odds of being trapped and running out of air in an enclosed space about 200,000 to 1. So your chances of being hurt in this way are pretty slim, but that doesn't mean you shouldn't be sensible.

The lowdown

Although it might not feel like it to a claustrophobe, small rooms, lifts, train platforms, football matches and rock concerts are all relatively safe places to be, and there's no reason to fear the closeness of walls and crowds, provided they're not getting steadily closer.

If you do suffer from panic attacks in places like this, you can comfortably learn to get around them using the same kinds of therapy exercises as are used for fears of heights and the dark. Little by little, you can learn to control your breathing, your physical responses and your feelings in ever-tighter spaces and crowds, until they bother you no more. And just as with the fear of heights, you can even try Virtual Reality simulations if jumping straight into the real thing proves difficult. So you've tried Guitar Hero . . . you've tried Rock Band . . . now try Rock Crowd Hero!

When the teacher picked me

'Usually I knew the material forward and backwards. I could have answered any question standing on my head. If I wasn't so terrified, I suppose I could have even been a show-off. But if she asked me (in front of the whole class), I might as well have been a baboon – the answers would fly out of my head and I would be a stuttering idiot. Sitting there with everybody watching me, the most I could ever say was "I don't know."'

The fear

Some of us are fine with the idea of standing in front of huge crowds of people. But others would happily bungee off a 200-foot bridge, or dive into a shoal of circling sharks, rather than experience the sheer terror of facing an audience. Shoved out on stage, or to the front of a class, a person like this will quite literally lose their voice. The mouth may open, but the words won't come out. They just stand there gaping like helpless goldfish pulled out of water, their weak limbs quaking with fear, feeling like they want to run, hide or cry. If that sounds like you, then you are one of the world's many, many sufferers of *glossophobia* – the fear of speaking (or trying to speak) in public.

The reality

*Glossophobia** is amazingly common – there are usually at least four or five kids in every school class that have it, and it's very common in adults too as you generally don't 'grow out' of *glossophobia*. It takes help or practice to get over it. This is because it's basically a type of social phobia – a fear of being watched, judged or sized up by other people (especially strangers, and especially large numbers of them).

So where does it come from, and what use is it? I mean, if fear of the dark, heights and dangerous animals helped keep our ancestors from being ambushed, what good is a fear of speaking to people? Wouldn't being able to speak to big groups have helped those early humans to communicate? The ones who were best at it, you'd think, could become chiefs, kings and emperors.** If speaking is that useful, what is this fear trying to protect us from? Being booed and pelted with rotten vegetables if we do badly?

Well, the answer is – nothing, really. There's no real danger involved in speaking to people. But the action of standing there and being watched can trigger a much

---

* Which sounds to me more like 'the fear of glossy magazines', or 'the fear of shiny paint'. But there you go.

** Even today, it's often the best speakers that become politicians, prime ministers and presidents. Well, with perhaps a few exceptions . . .

older and more useful fear – the fear of being surrounded, threatened and attacked by other people.

Throughout the animal world, and especially in primates (the group that includes humans, gorillas and chimpanzees), staring at someone is a signal of fighting or aggression. Even when we chat to people we trust and like, we don't stare them out while we talk. Instead, we shift the focus of our eyes around the other person's face – from their eyes to their mouth and nose and back again – and we glance away every so often during the conversation. (If you don't believe me, try it with a friend. Sit close to each other and just stare while you talk, without looking away, for one minute. You'll probably find you both start to feel really uncomfortable very quickly!) All of this helps to break up the eye contact, and reassures each person that the other is still friendly. Without it, a long burst of eye contact feels like the build-up to a scrap.

Now multiply that one staring pair of eyes by thirty, and you have some idea of why standing up to speak in front of a class can feel so unnerving. Multiply it by 500 or 1,000, and you see why it takes a lot of confidence to be on stage in a packed theatre. Even though the audience is (probably) quite friendly, the sensation is like being surrounded by an angry tribe, and all your brain wants to do is get you out of there. So that's what it prepares you to do. The old 'fight-or-flight' system we ran into earlier kicks in, making your heart rate increase, your breathing tight and rapid, your muscles tense, and your guts feel queasy (as blood is directed away from them). The whole time you're trying to speak or perform, your brain is saying 'OK – any minute now we leg it, right? Get ready . . . readyyy . . . readyyyyyyyyyy . . .'

For some people, this feels quite thrilling. But for *glossophobics*, it's absolutely terrifying.

But if you think about it, there really is nothing to be afraid of this time. Unlike the fear of water, heights and the dark, there's no real danger present at all. Even if you speak or perform really badly, it's not like the audience is going to *kill* you – the worst response you'll get is silence, booing, or rotten fruit and veg. None of these are pleasant, but none of them can actually harm you either.*

Happily, this also makes *glossophobia* a perfect example of a fear you can beat with simple practice. Since there's no real danger at all, it's much easier to work up from speaking to one, to two, to ten, to thirty people. Believe it or not, you can go from stage-phobic to star performer in no time!

---

* Except perhaps if they throw pineapples. Even a rotten pineapple could give you a nasty bruise if they haven't skinned it. But thankfully, it's also very difficult to smuggle a whole pineapple into a classroom or theatre. Believe me, I've tried.

The chances

The odds of being killed by a classroom or theatre full of people just because you're speaking or performing to them? Zero.

Unless you're really, *really* bad . . .

No, really – it's zero. Just winding you up.

The lowdown

The fear of being 'in the spotlight' is extremely common, and, to those that suffer from it, extremely powerful. But it's also extremely easy to work around, given a bit of effort. Since there's no real danger involved at all, it's just a matter of convincing your brain that you don't need the 'fight-or-flight' system to kick in when you're speaking or performing before people. How do you do that? Practise!

There are lots of ways of working around your fears and building your confidence before audiences. The most direct (and powerful) way is to join a school, church or community speaking group, where you can be coached on how to give speeches. At first, you may practise alone or with one or two people. Then, as you get more confident, you can work up to larger and larger groups, until before you know it you're speaking to whole school assemblies, church congregations or community groups! The best thing is that in many cases you get to talk about whatever you want, whether it's 'Ten Ways to Make a Better World', 'My Love of Dinosaurs', or 'Why Xbox Will Always Be Inferior to the Nintendo Wii'!

If that doesn't sound like any kind of fun, then you

can get experience with speaking in front of audiences without speaking *directly* to them. In acting or debating clubs, you can practise talking to small groups of people while watched by an audience, but without having to look straight at them. Plus the act of concentrating on your lines or on the argument will help distract you from the many watching eyes. When you get really good at it, you might even forget the audience is there!

And if you really can't imagine *speaking* in front of crowds at all, then you can work up to it (or at the very least gain a lot more confidence) by trying other types of performance instead. Ever wanted to dance? How about play guitar, or sing? Learning a performing art of any kind will help you get over your fears of an audience if you eventually take it to the stage.

So if you're one of the world's many perform-o-phobes, don't worry – the 'treatment' for it may turn out to be the most fun you've ever had. The prescription looks like this:

Take a handul of guitar, acting or dance lessons, *rock* a roomful of people with your mad new skills, and call me in the morning!

Fear Fact:

Famous actor Mel Gibson was so nervous before his first school play that he had to do his role sitting down. His legs and body were too weak for him to stand.

6 The Unknown

Fear of Fear Itself

So we've worked out that people are afraid of lots of different things for lots of different reasons. A few fears are built into our brains from birth to help protect us from harm. We learn most of the rest through scary experiences of our own, or from hearing scary stories from others. But the one thing that ties almost all of these fears together is . . . uncertainty or not-knowing.

If someone moves a hand slowly toward your face, you just sit there and watch them do it. But if they sneak up on you and quickly pass a hand in front of your face from behind, you flinch.

Why? Because it happened too quickly for your brain to work out what was going on. For the first split-second after the hand appears, your brain doesn't know if it's a hand, a bird or a flying rock in your face. So it triggers an automatic reaction – your flinch reflex – to quickly jerk your head away (and shield your eyes, partly or fully closing them) until it has had a chance to work out what you're dealing with. So this reflex is a kind of *automatic* fear, lasting a fraction of a second, which kicks in when your brain doesn't know what's going on.

A similar thing happens if you slowly place a fake spider on someone's leg while they watch. Unless they're *seriously* arachnophobic, hardly anyone would flinch or jump if they saw you do this. But place it there while they're not looking, and even someone who *likes* spiders may jump and hastily brush it off. Again, in the first split second after they spot it, the brain can't work out how it got there, or exactly what it is (a fake spider or a real one). So the person jumps and swats at it as an automatic response to something unexpected and unknown. The same thing happens with sudden loud bangs, with sudden bursts of music in horror movies, or with sudden flashes of movement at the edge of your vision.[*] 'Whawuzzthat?!?!' your brain says. And until it gets an answer, flinching and fear are the standard responses.

In a way, all fear responses share this link to uncertainty and not-knowing. But while flinching happens in a fraction of a second, anxiety, dread and panic are reactions to the unknown that can build up over minutes, hours, days or years.

---

[*] It also works with hamsters placed carefully on the heads of balding uncles. I did this once with my Uncle Eddie at a family party, as he sat and chatted to my Uncle Peter on the sofa. Peter didn't see me put my pet hamster on there, but he jumped out of his skin when Eddie's 'wig' leaped off his head and scurried across the carpet. Which got a good laugh out of pretty much everyone in the room.

Once the flinch response is over a person's reaction will depend on what they know and how they feel about spiders. *Arachnophobes*, not knowing whether or not the spider on their leg (or – if they've just brushed it off in a panic – on the floor) is venomous or whether it will jump at them, may immediately panic or become hysterical as a second, more powerful fear response kicks in. But an *arachnophile* – who knows it *isn't* dangerous, and *won't* jump – may not panic at all.

Most people, perhaps, would be somewhere in the middle. Not certain whether the spider is dangerous or not (but noticing it isn't jumping or trying to bite them yet), they may be nervous or anxious, but not terrified. The only difference between the three people is *how much they know* about the spider, and *how uncertain they are* about what's likely to happen next.

The fears in this final section are special, as they all relate to things that are scary *mostly because* they're unknown or unknowable. Spiders, earthquakes, lightning, dentists and diseases can be pretty scary, but at least we know and understand what they are. Not so for ghosts, monsters, aliens, death and dying. These things are, for many people, mysterious and difficult to understand. They sit within the Big Book of Scary, Bad Stuff* that has confused and terrified people for thousands of years. But if you think about it, earthquakes, lightning and many other things were, until

---

* This book doesn't really exist, of course. Although that is a *cracking* title . . .

fairly recently, in that book too. Before we had science to help explain what these things were, people thought they were the work of demons, evil spirits or angry gods. Now that we know more about earthquakes and lightning, we don't fear them nearly as much. We might not be able to predict when they'll strike, but we know why they happen, and we know they're not *trying* to get us, even when they do.

Now here's the funny thing. Our brains make us fear things we don't recognize, can't expect, or don't understand. But as we've already seen, learning more about the things we fear can help us understand them and, eventually, lose our fear of them altogether.

So being afraid of something *just because* you don't understand it – but then refusing to *try* to understand it – is like being afraid of fear itself!

So let's try and take a few more things out of that Big Book of Scary, Bad Stuff, as we head into the final chapter and deeeeeep into . . .

. . . the unknooooown.

The terrible turtle monster

In Japan, people still speak of the Kappa, a strange monster which looks like a cross between a monkey, a frog and a turtle. About the height of a small child, it swims like a fish in water, but on land it walks upright on webbed feet, like a human. Weirdest of all, it has a bowl-like dent in the top of its head filled with water – the source of its enormous strength and power.

Some Kappa, it's said, are truly evil. They kidnap children and eat people, sucking their victim's entrails out through their bottom. The best way to defeat a Kappa is to bow to it, as all Kappa (even the evil ones) are very polite and will bow back, spilling the precious, strength-giving water from the pool atop their head.

The fear

As scary as lightning, spiders, dentists and darkened rooms can be, at least we know what they are. Monsters, on the other hand, are different. They might be animals, they might be mutant people, but we don't really know what they are. (If we did, then we could call them something else, like a bear, a dinosaur, or a big, hairy person.) And that makes them scarier than anything.

Thousands of mysterious beasts and monsters have been sighted all over the world, and they seem to date back as far as human history itself. There are human-like monsters with huge, hairy bodies and terrifying strength. There are bat-like monsters that swoop out of the night to suck the blood of animals and children. Ship-sinking sea monsters with writhing tentacles, man-eating dog-beasts with terrible fangs, hideous cat-beasts with horrible claws . . . the list goes on and on. Scientists say most monsters are just figments of our imagination. But with so many monsters spotted in so many places, so many times, how can they be sure? Who's to say there really isn't something lurking under your bed, waiting to eat you just as soon as you nod off to sleep?

The reality

Who's to say there isn't a monster under your bed? Well, me for starters. And pretty much every scientist in the world.

It's true that scientists don't know everything (and

they don't pretend to either – one of the great things about science is that it allows you to be happily uncertain about things). But what they do know is based on proof and evidence. And as far as monsters go, there just ain't much of either about.

What little evidence there is for monsters tends to be pretty sketchy – usually a grainy, out-of-focus photograph or a set of footprints indicating that the monster was *just here*, and you *just missed it*. Most monster 'proof' comes in the form of stories or eyewitness accounts from people who have seen them (like the story of the Yeti attack above). Now you could say that's proof enough for you, but, for scientists, this isn't really good enough. Dodgy photographs and tracks make it unclear whether you've captured evidence of a monster or a normal animal (or person) under weird lighting conditions.

Take, for example, the Yeti, otherwise known as the Abominable Snowman. Huge, hairy ape-man creatures like this have been talked about for centuries, in countries all over the world. In Asia, it's called the Yeti. In North America, it's called Bigfoot (or Sasquatch), in South America the Ucu. Even Australia (where you'd think it'd be a bit warm for hairy man-apes), there's one called the Yowie. In the past, some scientists thought that maybe there was some truth to the stories. Maybe these beasts were really the prehistoric, pre-human survivors of another age – massive hairy cavemen that never died out. But after years of searching and collecting evidence, all we've turned up are blurred photographs that could easily be normal people (possibly in fake Yeti-suits!) or huge footprints in snow and mud that could simply have enlarged as they decayed, the edges falling inward over time to give the illusion of a huge footprint.

Similarly, some scientists used to think the famous Loch Ness Monster might be a Plesiosaur – a huge aquatic reptile* that somehow survived in a Scottish loch for millions of years after all the others had died out. Maybe they even survived in lakes elsewhere too, since Nessie-like monsters have also been reported in lakes in Africa (where it's called the Mokele-mbele) and China (home of the 'Heavenly Lake Monster'). But in the absence of anything but stories and dodgy photographs that *could* be fins, which is more likely? That families of massive reptiles have survived almost unseen since the Cretaceous Age, or that the locals are mistaken?

Now you could say, 'OK – so there's no evidence yet, but that doesn't mean there never will be.' That's true. Science never rules out the possibility of monsters existing. And it could be that some so-called 'monsters' are really just animals that we already know about (but the locals don't), or even rare species we've never seen before. In both cases, eyewitness sightings of these 'monsters' might be exaggerated because they're so unusual and difficult

---

* But not – as many people think – a dinosaur, although they died out around the same time as most of the true dinosaurs. Pterodactyls aren't dinosaurs either. Or rather, *weren't* dinosaurs, since they've gone too. Sadly.

to explain. Experiencing the unknown can play tricks on your senses and memory, making things seem bigger (and scarier) than they really are.

So some monsters may just be normal animals, others may be hoaxes or tricks created on purpose to fool people, and perhaps most are just stories made up to explain away unusual events (like escaped zoo animals killing livestock, or strange tracks formed in snow or mud by wind and weather).

The chances

Since monsters are either imagined, created by hoaxes or not actually monsters at all, then your chances of being hurt or killed by a monster are pretty much exactly ZERO. I say 'pretty much', as it's possible that your 'monster' could turn out to be something like an escaped big cat – and one of those could certainly do you damage. But then it's not really a monster that's attacking you, is it? It's . . . well . . . a cat. In any case, escaped cats don't generally hide under beds or in wardrobes, so you're still in the clear.

The lowdown

Whether imagined, faked or just a case of mistaken animal identity, we can safely say that monsters are not a threat to your health or survival. Even if (and this is a big 'if') some 'monsters' turn out to be huge, dangerous animal species that we thought were extinct – like dinosaurs,

Pterodactyls and Sabre-toothed Tigers – then they're probably still not much of a danger to you. Think about it: if it's been that hard to catch a glimpse of these beasts over decades and centuries, then it's pretty unlikely that you'll just stumble upon one . . . or have one stumble upon you.

In the Himalayas, you've far more to fear from freezing to death and falling down crevasses than from a ravenous Yeti. And if you ever meet one, you can tell him I said that.

Fear Facts:

Monsters Around the World

The Loch Ness Monster: Reported sightings of the world-famous Loch Ness Monster (or 'Nessie', as the locals call her) date back almost 2,000 years. But interest in Nessie really peaked in 1972, when a diver captured what looked like a plesiosaur's flipper in an underwater photograph. Then in 1987 a team of scientists used 19 boats with sonar scanners to sweep the loch looking for her. Alas – no luck and no proof. But since they left a good third of the loch unscanned, the locals say Nessie (or a family of Nessies) could still be there, hiding.

The Yeti: This 8-foot-tall, shaggy, grey man-ape has apparently been roaming the mountain passes of Nepal and Tibet for centuries, and the Himalayan Sherpa people know and fear the Yeti (or rather, Yetis, as they believe there are many of them) as an evil spirit. European mountain climbers have also reported spotting Yetis or Yeti footprints on icy glaciers and peaks never before climbed. But beyond a few sketchy footprint photographs, there's no solid, hairy evidence of them yet.

The Beast of Bodmin: This large leopard- or panther-like cat has been spotted thousands of times a year by the residents of Bodmin Moor in Devon, south-west England. The beast is said to roam the moor year-round, killing hundreds of sheep and cows. Sightings of footprints, dead livestock and the animal itself only date back to the 1980s, and some think it's possible that the 'Beast' is actually a family of big cats that was released into the wild by a private owner around that time. One piece of video evidence does exist, showing a distant, dark, panther-like animal stalking the moor. But no one has ever seen the Beast of Bodmin ('Bob' to his mates) up close, let alone captured it.

The Kraken: This enormous squid-like sea monster, thought to be between 15 and 65 metres long, has terrorized the seas of northern Europe since Viking times. Scientists used to dismiss the Kraken as a complete myth, but since the recent discovery of a new species of giant squid – the colossal Squid – many are not so sure. Colossal Squid may reach up to 15m in length, and a 'baby' specimen measuring 10m and weighing almost 500kg was captured by a fishing boat near Antarctica in 2007.

The Ahool: Named after their shrieking cry, Ahools reportedly look like monkeys with massive, 5m-wide bat wings. They live in caves in the rainforests of Indonesia, and locals say they swoop out at night to catch fish in their claw-like hands. Many scientists think these may be exaggerated sightings of flying foxes – large, furry bats that live in the region.

The Kongamoto: Another huge bat-like creature, this time living in Zambia, Africa. Locals say it has a hairless, reptilian body, and a long beak with teeth (much like the now-extinct Pterodactyl). They also say that it swoops down on fishermen and capsizes their boats, and causes death to anyone who looks into its eyes. But there's no real evidence of a Pterodactyl – or a flying-bat monster – living in Africa.

The Bunyip: The Australian Aboriginal people say the Bunyip – a large dog-like creature with webbed feet and walrus-like tusks – lives in riverbeds and watering holes throughout the bush, coming out at night to eat any animal that comes near. No real-live Bunyips have been found yet, and most zoologists doubt they exist. But then again, they also doubted the existence of the Platypus, which was painted and talked about by Aborigines for generations before sceptical scientists finally found one.

The Chupacabra: This bear-sized, lizard-skinned, dog-faced, snake-fanged vampire lives in South America, where it sucks the blood from pigs, horses and goats. Oh, and it also has porcupine quills down its back and hops like a kangaroo. Most zoologists consider this one *waaaaay* too weird to exist – and there's certainly never been any evidence of it, other than livestock that could easily have been killed by other animals (or people) instead.

The Mongolian Death Worm: An enormous blood-filled worm which lives in the dunes of the Mongolian desert. It can kill you by spitting venom at you, or by shocking you like an electric eel. None have ever been found by zoologists. Possibly because they've all been eaten by mutant Mongolian blackbirds. But, hey – that's just my theory.

The Mothman: A 7-foot-tall humanoid monster with huge moth wings and glowing red eyes, sighted in parts of West Virginia, USA, since the 1960s. Some say it's an evil sprit. Others say it's a failed experiment – an evil mutant animal escaped from a local army base. I say the locals should eat less cheese before bed.

The world's first alien abduction?

Shortly after 10 p.m. on 19 September, 1961, American holidaymakers Betty and Barney Hill were driving home from their trip to Canada. Suddenly, they both noticed a bright star which appeared out of nowhere and seemed to be following them. Barney thought it might be an aeroplane or satellite, but when the light remained Betty grabbed a pair of binoculars to view the object, and Barney stopped the car for a closer look. It appeared to be a large, glowing pancake with a double row of windows.

Then Barney noticed there were others looking at them through the windows and became terrified, convinced somehow that he and Betty were about to be captured. They raced off, accompanied by a 'beeping' sound from behind the car, which seemed to make them drowsy. After a second burst of the beeping sound, they became fully awake, and found themselves several miles away from where they had spotted the object. Unable to remember what had happened, they drove home.

Shortly after the UFO incident, Betty began having nightmares in which she was taken aboard the UFO and examined by little humanoid beings, while Barney began to suffer from exhaustion, high blood pressure, ulcers, and a strange ring of warts near his groin . . .

The fear

Since the first reports in the late 1960s, there have been millions of accounts of people being abducted by aliens. The victims are usually either hijacked outside their homes by UFOs, or taken from their beds in the middle of the night. These alien kidnap victims (or 'alien abductees') often remember very little of what happened, only recalling later on how they were taken inside spaceships, injected with needles, and poked and prodded by alien 'doctors'. Many recall waking up in their beds, paralysed and unable to move, to find hideous creatures standing before them.

Creatures with huge heads and eyes, spindly limbs and greyish skin, watching them with silent, evil curiosity.

What do they want? Are they scouts leading an invasion of our planet? Are they conducting some bizarre alien experiment on us all? Are they creating a race of freakish alien–human half-breeds? Whatever the case, it seems we puny humans are no match for their superior technology and intelligence. Their spaceships fly around undetected by armies and air forces. They control our minds and our bodies, plucking us from our homes at will. And we're powerless to understand or resist. So run for your lives – the body-snatchers are coming!

The reality

OK, OK, calm down. They're not coming just yet. In fact, they may *never* come, and there's very little evidence that they've ever been here at all.

Despite the millions of alien abduction stories that have surfaced over the last half-century, not one has provided a scrap of solid evidence that it ever happened. No alien souvenirs swiped from spaceships, no photographs or video footage of their captors, and no outside witnesses to back up stories. So all we have to go on are the victims' own words and memories. What little 'evidence' has been offered so far has been sketchy at best. Blurred photographs of frisbee-like objects or wobbling lights in the sky, strange bruises and marks on the bodies of alien abductees, and so on. Looked at like this, which seems more likely: that evil aliens are kidnapping people all the time, largely unnoticed by the rest of us, or that these 'alien kidnap' victims are misleading us (or themselves)?

That's not to say that aliens definitely don't exist. Having no proof isn't the same thing as proving there's nothing there. In fact, given the unimaginably huge size of the Universe, and the number of planets in it that could support life (scientists estimate that there could be thousands of suitable planets in our galaxy alone), it would be surprising if it turned out we were all alone. But while there might well be life elsewhere in the Universe, it might not be complex life like us. For almost all of the Earth's 4.5 billion-year history, all that lived here were simple, single-celled organisms like bacteria – complex life only evolved within the last few hundred million years. So if we do find life elsewhere, there's a good chance it won't be at the same stage of evolution as life on Earth. Or to put it another way, life could be common, but complex life like humans could be very rare – even unique – in the Universe.

Even assuming there was complex life out there somewhere on another planet, that's not to say they have civilizations and technology, or spacecraft. We humans only came up with those things within the last few thousand years (for manned spacecraft, only about 50 years ago, and only a few of those have ever made it more than a few miles away from the Earth). What's more, we already know there are no alien civilizations in our solar system, and the nearest solar systems capable of supporting them are billions and trillions of miles away. So even if 'they' are out there, it's unlikely that alien civilizations would manage to bridge the distance between us to come and visit. (And if they had, then you'd think after all that effort getting here they might do something a bit more useful than kidnapping American farmers at random.)

Of course, that doesn't necessarily mean all of the so-called alien abductees are lying, or that all UFO sightings are hoaxes. Many (if not most) alien abduction stories can be explained by medical conditions like temporal lobe epilepsy and sleep paralysis. Both of these conditions can make victims feel as if they're paralysed and trapped inside their own bodies. They can also make sufferers hallucinate (or seem to see, as if in a waking dream) humanoid figures right in front of them, and interfere with memory formation so that it seems like the person has 'lost' minutes or hours of their lives (which in reality they just can't remember).

Even for those who don't suffer from these conditions, many otherwise normal people often experience hallucinations just as they drift off to sleep (*hypnogogic* hallucinations), or just after waking up (*hypnopompic* hallucinations). At these times, the brain becomes more suggestible and prone to confusion – which is the very thing hypnotists exploit when they make people sleepy and get them to do funny things on stage. In fact, many abductees (including Betty and Barney Hill, whom we met in the opening story) actually 'recall' their alien encounters under hypnosis, which can create a very unreliable mixture of real and imagined memories.

So while some 'alien victims' are hoaxers and liars, perhaps most actually believe that it really happened to them – for reasons they don't themselves understand.

Happily, this means also that neither they, nor we, need to fear an alien attack any time soon.

The chances

If you believed every alien abduction report was true – and there are thousands of them every year in the USA alone – then you'd have to accept that about 2% of the world's population is 'taken' by aliens annually. That's well over a hundred million people. As the late, great astronomer Carl Sagan once said, 'You'd think someone would have noticed all that UFO traffic.'

But since there's no proof that alien abductions have ever happened at all, your chances of being kidnapped, harmed or killed by aliens are – as far as we know – precisely zero. Hooray!

The lowdown

Based on all the evidence we have, aliens may well exist somewhere in the Universe, but none have been here yet. So until the day an advanced alien civilization does surprise us by arriving in a mothership to claim the planet for themselves, we can safely say that aliens are nothing to be afraid of.

All those scary alien abduction stories can be explained by a simple fear of the unknown, combined with mistakes, hallucinations, medical conditions, and the influence of books, movies and the media.

'Abduction' stories didn't start with aliens either. Throughout history, there have been stories of children and adults being 'taken' or attacked by demons or monsters. These stories share many of the same features as those of alien abductees – such as being 'attacked' in bed, in the middle of the night, being paralysed or frozen, and being taken up into the sky. All that has happened is that aliens have become the new demons – a newer, more modern way to explain the same feelings of fear and powerlessness that people get when they see a strange light they can't explain, or half-wake from a dream to find themselves unable to move.

Ever since the 1960s, books, movies and the media have helped spread common ideas of what aliens might look like and how they might behave. All over the world, people report seeing the same kinds of grey, spindly, big-eyed aliens because that's how the earliest stories of the 1960s described them. Alien attack stories are like high-tech, modern monster-myths that have spread around the world, becoming folk tales for everyone who has seen the movies or read the books. All of these ideas just give a name and a shape to our shared fear of the unfamiliar and unknown.

So don't worry – the alien body-snatchers aren't coming to get you. At least not yet . . .

Fear Facts:

Famous Hollywood Aliens

E.T. (From *E.T.– the Extra-Terrestrial*) A small, brown, wrinkly alien with a glowing finger, healing powers, and an extendable neck. Looks a lot like a Hoover with eyes. Which could be confusing for them, if aliens like this ever came to Earth.

Chewbacca (*Star Wars*) A tall, hairy member of an alien race called the Wookies, who hangs out with Han Solo on his spaceship. Can understand English, but only replies in growls and gurgles.* Looks a lot like a tall man in a hairy suit. If the world were invaded by Wookies, we'd soon run out of shampoo.

Xenomorphs and Predators (*Alien, Aliens, Alien 3, Predator, Predator 2, Alien vs Predator . . .*) One is a huge, hideous, parasitic monster which eats people's brains and incubates its young inside human bodies. The other is a dreadlocked, crab-faced, stealth-suited killer

---

* Which, confusingly, Han Solo seems to understand perfectly. Perhaps he went to Wookie language classes at some point.

which hunts humans for sport. If these things exist, we'd better hope they never find us!

The Martians (*War of the Worlds*) Small, squishy, large-headed aliens with superior intelligence and technology to ours. They stride around in huge war machines, exterminating humans with heat rays, while keeping a few of us in reserve to harvest our blood. Luckily, common Earth bacteria are deadly to them. Let's hear it for the bacteria – yet again!

Doctor Spock (*Star Trek*) An extremely clever, human-like alien with pointy ears and dodgy eyebrows. His mother was human, but his father was from an alien race called the Vulcans. He has superhuman strength, he can read minds, and he can knock people out by pinching them. Would be a great mate to have at school, as he could do your maths homework *and* fend off bullies. Brilliant.

The haunted tower

Today the Tower of London is one of the most popular tourist destinations in Europe. The central tower is almost 1,000 years old, and was built by order of William the Conqueror to celebrate his victorious conquest of England in 1066. Since that time it has been expanded, fortified and used by various monarchs as a fortress, a palace and a prison. It is also a place of death – hundreds of prisoners have been executed within its walls, the last as recently as 1940. Little wonder, then, that the Tower has also been the location of more ghost sightings and encounters than perhaps any other place in the world.

In 1483 two young princes were murdered in the Tower, and their ghosts were said to haunt it until their bones were discovered in 1674 and reburied in Westminster Abbey. One of King Henry VIII's more unfortunate wives, Anne Boleyn, was beheaded in the Tower courtyard, as was the treasonous Guy Fawkes. Their spirits, too, are said to walk the grounds. A mysterious 'White Lady' waves at visiting schoolchildren from windows, and terrified Tower guards once spoke of an evil presence that attacks lone patrollers by night. The invisible spectre, it was said, caused a crushing sensation in your chest, or tried to strangle you with your own clothes. At least one guard reportedly died of shock when he encountered it ...

The fear

Oooooooo, creepy! There's nothing like a good ghost story to get your heart beating faster and send chills down your spine. And there are certainly plenty of stories out there to choose from. There are stories about haunted houses – with creepy noises, creaking doors and furniture shifted by an invisible presence. Stories about séances – where psychic mediums fall into trances and become possessed by the ghosts of the dead, while the table shakes and the room lights flicker frighteningly on and off. Stories about curious kids who play with Ouija boards, asking questions of evil spirits – who toy with them ... and tell them only of their own deaths.

Worst of all, there are stories of actual ghost sightings. Horrible apparitions with dead, lifeless eyes and grasping hands. Spirits seeking revenge for their untimely deaths. Floating phantoms who haunt the hallways of places where they once lived. Ghastly spectres who sob, scream, and scare the poor living to death – where they join the ghostly hordes and live on in limbo to terrify us all. WOOOOOOOOOO!!

WOoo^OOO-O^{OO}o_ooo-oo^{OO}OoO ...

The reality

... OOOOOOO!!! WOO-OO—

(Cough.) Ahem! All right, enough of that.

As fears go, ghosts are a funny one. We love to scare ourselves with stories about them, yet most of us won't admit we really believe in them. Not *really*.

But then where do all those stories come from? It seems difficult to ignore all those creepy stories when there are so many of them out there, unexplained ...

Few of us have ever had a ghostly encounter ourselves, yet everyone seems to know someone who has. There are those who say they've seen one or heard one clunking around their house or floating through their bedroom. There are those who have been to see mediums, or messed about with Ouija* boards, and say they were convinced they were communicating with the dead. Then there are books and movies about ghosts and hauntings – all 'based on a true story'. And what about all those programmes on TV where real-life 'ghost hunters' visit haunted places, capturing strange, ghostly happenings on night-vision cameras and special spirit-sensing instruments?

Stick all this together, and there seems to be quite a bit of evidence for ghosts and spirits, and plenty of fuel for the widespread fear of them – otherwise known as *phasmophobia*. But how well does the evidence really hold up?

The truth is, just as with monsters and aliens, there are plenty of stories, but the evidence doesn't hold up well at all. In fact, in over a century of research into parapsychology (the study of psychic abilities and life after death, using science-like methods), there is no proof at all that ghosts and spirits exist. Of course, that doesn't mean we've proved that ghosts *don't* exist either. But since we can explain most of these scary goings-on in other ways, we're pretty sure that there's no real reason to be afraid of them.

Time and time again, scientists have demonstrated that

---

* Although most people call these 'Ouiji' or 'Wee-jee' boards, the correct name is actually 'Ouija'. They get their name from the French and German words for 'yes' – 'oui', and 'ja' – since in addition to the letters of the alphabet, all Ouija boards also display the words 'yes' and 'no', so that the ghost/spirit/person pushing the glass can answer simple questions. The wittiest ghosts typically answer 'Is there anybody theeeerrre?' with a 'No'.

mediums (people who claim they can talk to spirits or the dead) are either fakes or – at the very least – failures. When mediums hold 'sittings' or 'readings' with those who have lost a loved one, they often give details of the dead person's life – guided, they say, by the spirits of the dead themselves. But while their 'readings' might seem accurate to the listener, they're actually using clever word tricks and clues to guess the details. For example, the medium might begin like this:

'I see a red bicycle, the letter 'K' and a young woman . . .'

'Well,' says the listener, 'my mother's sister was called Catherine, but I don't think she rode a bike . . .'

'Yes, yes – Catherine. She's here now. And she did have a bicycle when she was younger – you were just too young to remember. I'm also seeing a black dog . . . or possibly a cat'

'That's amazing!' says the listener, 'Auntie Catherine did have a cat – a big black one! And now you mention it, I think she and my mother did ride bikes when they were little . . .'

So the listener sees 'the letter K' as a correct guess at 'Catherine', even though the medium was actually *wrong* about it! And the chances of the listener knowing *someone* connected to her late mother whose name began with *either* a 'C' *or* a 'K' are pretty high. Likewise, since *most* people ride bikes when they're young, and *most* people keep pets, the chances that this person 'used to ride a bicycle' and had a 'dog . . . or possibly a cat' are very high too. In strict tests, scientists have shown that medium's guesses are no better than anyone else's. They're wrong at least as often as they're right. So if they're not faking their chats with the dead, then they're really not very good at it.

As for séances and Ouija boards, they don't hold up well to strict testing either. The wobbling table in a séance isn't caused by a ghost, but by the host lifting it with a foot (or sometimes using a special 'hands-free' body harness) from underneath, and lights flicker because the host has set up special switches to trigger them. Ouija boards, on the other hand, spell out answers because one or more people touching the glass are pushing it (whether they realize it or not) towards certain letters. The movement is caused by a mind trick called the ideomotor reflex,* not by some mischievous poltergeist.

Finally, we have the full-on ghostly visits, visions and hauntings. How do we explain those? Well, not one case that has ever been seriously investigated has given any permanent evidence that a ghost was present. Sometimes people will report seeing, hearing or feeling similar things in the same places. But they always fail to capture any photographs, sound recordings or video clips that will back up the story. Which seems to suggest that the ghostly sights, sounds and sensations may be in the haunted *head* rather than the haunted *house* . . .

Just as with alien abduction stories, there's some evidence that medical conditions such as temporal lobe

---

* See page 249 for how you can test this out for yourself – it's great for freaking out your friends!

epilepsy can cause hallucinations that make it look as if there are strange people in the room. So where some people with this condition see 'aliens', others see 'ghosts'.

Some researchers have also found that strong electromagnetic fields can make people – even people without temporal lobe epilepsy – hallucinate, by affecting the normal workings of their brains. Certain electrical waves, applied to certain parts of the brain, can make you feel as if there's someone standing beside you, or even touching you. So it may be that many 'haunted' houses are just old houses with dodgy electrical wiring that floods certain spots of the house with electromagnetic fields. If you walk into that spot your brain gets affected, and you 'see' or 'feel' the ghost.

There is even a type of sound that can cause your eyeballs to vibrate, and make it look as if there's a hazy, floating shape at the edge of your vision. This type of sound, called *infrasound*, has a frequency too low for us to hear* so it affects us without our realizing it. Infrasound can be created in a number of different ways, including by the massive wind turbines used to generate electricity. So if this theory is correct, maybe ghost 'sightings' will go up along with all the new windmills we're building!

In any case, all of these explanations seem more likely

---

* Whales and elephants, however, use infrasound to communicate all the time. So either their eyeballs are vibration-proof, or they're constantly seeing ghosts and freaking each other out. If so, I wonder what whale and elephant ghosts look like? Would they have trunks, or flippers and tails? Hmmmmmm . . .

than the alternative – that evil spirits linger on after death to terrorize us, but leave no evidence beyond a few sketchy ghost stories.

The chances

The odds of being dragged into the land of the dead by a ghost or evil spirit – as far as we know – are nil. You could, of course, scare yourself (or someone else) to death if you (or they) had a heart problem, but you couldn't blame that on a ghost. Not even if you were dressed like one.

The lowdown

Ghosts, as far as we know, simply do not exist, and pose no danger to you, me or anyone else. Ghost sightings and stories are just another example of people seeing, hearing or feeling things they can't easily explain, and slapping a 'supernatural' label on it to try and make sense of it all. Some ghostly sensations can be explained by simple trickery, others by medical conditions like temporal lobe epilepsy, and still others by the rare (but real) effects of electromagnetic fields and soundwaves on the eyes, ears and brain. Whatever the case, ghosts are best thought of as hallucinations and tricks of the mind, rather than evil forces out to get us.

It's easy to be freaked out by something you don't expect and can't easily explain. But that doesn't mean you have to *stay* freaked out. Look a little deeper, and you'll almost always find a simple explanation for the eerie knocking sound you heard in the walls, the cold shiver you felt as you stood in that cellar, or the blurred face you're sure you saw at the window of that deserted house. Instead of giving in to your panic and your fear of the 'unknown', think about it or investigate a little more. Chances are you'll soon find that the *real* explanation – a swelling metal pipe in the walls, a draught of cold air in the cellar, or a weird lighting effect in the window – isn't scary at all.

Make your own poltergeist!

'Poltergeist' is a German word meaning 'knocking ghosts'. These mischievous spirits are famous for making knocking noises and moving things around in people's houses. Some people also believe that spirits move the upturned glass on a Ouija board. On a Ouija board, everyone touches the glass but no one pushes it – yet the glass, spookily, moves itself, as if possessed by a poltergeist.

In truth, the glass-touchers *are* pushing – they just don't know it. Just by looking at a letter on the board, one of the touchers begins to push the glass unconsciously towards it. Then, as the glass moves towards the letter, the others help propel it and stop it, because they're unconsciously reacting to the first toucher's motion.

In certain circumstances, if you think about a movement and you're relaxed, the movement becomes real as your body responds in tiny ways you can hardly detect. This is called the *ideomotor reflex*.

You can test it with a pendulum. A necklace with a heavy pendant will do nicely. or, failing that, a conker tied on a string. It doesn't really matter as long as it can swing freely.

Wrap the string or chain around the base of your middle finger, then raise your elbow to shoulder level and hold the pendulum over a table so that the bob (pendant, conker, whatever) doesn't touch the surface. Now try to keep your hand as still as you can, but at the same time, look at the bob and imagine it moving to and fro. First try left to right – keep your hand still but keep thinking about it. Eventually the bob will start to move just as you imagine it. Now imagine it stopping. It will! Then try back and forth, then clockwise circles, then anti-clockwise. Watch it go! Is it a ghost?

No, it's you. Try as you might to keep your hand steady, your brain is transferring your imagined movement to your muscles, and they're responding with tiny contractions to start the motion. It doesn't feel like you're moving it, but you are.

Excellent. Well done. Now go and freak out your friends.

Not quite gone . . .

Rare as they are, real-life cases of people coming 'back from the dead' (or rather, being mistaken for dead) can and do happen.

In 1977 a hearse crashed into an undertaker's shop, the coffin flying out of the car and through a plate-glass window. Minutes later the 'corpse' stepped out of the wreckage and into the street – the crash having roused him from a coma.

In 1994 an 86-year-old American woman spent over an hour in a body bag before a morgue worker noticed that the bag was breathing. And in 1996, two morgue workers in Havana, Cuba, were playing chess on the night shift when a body beside them sat up and moved the bishop three squares. In both cases, the 'deceased' had suffered a heart attack and been mistakenly pronounced dead.

The fear

Death and dying are the ultimate big-scary-unknowns. Everybody eventually dies, but no one comes back to tell us what it was like. So in the absence of real knowledge, our fearful imaginations are left to run riot about how bad death and dying might be.

Can you 'catch' death from dying people, like you catch a disease? Or does death come to 'get' you, like a monster or a ghost? When it comes, do you fight it – struggling to stay in your body while someone (or something) tries to pull you away? Does it hurt? What if the doctors make a mistake, and they bury or burn you alive? And once you are dead and buried, what's *that* like? Do you lie there in the grave feeling cold, hungry or lonely? When will it happen? In 100 years? 50 years? Sooner?

The reality

Death and dying are scary to most people, because so much about them is uncertain or unknown. This raises a lot of questions that we have trouble answering, and not knowing the answers can make us even more afraid.

The truth is, we may never know for sure – while we're still alive – how death feels. But we do know quite a bit about what happens to our *bodies* during and after death. And that – at least – can answer some of these questions, and make the whole thing seem a bit less scary.

For starters, we know that death isn't a disease or a

monster that comes to 'get' you. It's a natural process that affects our bodies just as it affects flowers, trees, insects and other forms of life. When we die, our bodies stop moving, and we stop eating, drinking, growing and communicating with those around us. Then our bodies are recycled and absorbed back into the earth, air and water of the environment. If our bodies are cremated (or burned), our scattered ashes feed and fertilize the earth. If our bodies are buried, then insects, worms and bacteria* convert our bodies into nutrients, and these nutrients feed growing plants and animals for thousands of years after we die. So death forms part of a natural cycle that keeps all forms of life on Earth thriving and surviving.

Could we be buried alive by mistake? Well, no – not really. While this has certainly happened in the past, it's almost impossible nowadays. In the years before modern medicine, doctors or tribal healers would declare someone dead if they stopped breathing, or their hearts stopped beating. But we now know that a person can stop breathing (or even have their hearts stopped) for several minutes without dying – in some rare cases even longer. So doctors look for signs of brain activity instead of just breathing and heartbeat, using a machine that measures electrical signals in the brain, called an Electro-Encephalogram (or EEG). If there is still activity in the brain, the doctors will keep working to bring you back to life. Only when all signs of life

---

* See? There go those bacteria being helpful again!

in the brain are gone (or when the breathing and heartbeat can't be restored after a long time trying) does the doctor pronounce someone dead.

We also know that being dead doesn't hurt, and you won't feel cold or hungry in the grave either. Pain, hunger, and sensitivity to temperature are all functions of a living body, designed to keep it alive, and they need living nerves to be transmitted and felt. So once your body has died, you can't feel pain, hunger or cold any more.

When we see death in movies, or read about it in stories, the dying person is often shown fighting for their last breath and struggling desperately to stay alive. But in reality, only a fraction of the thousands of people who meet death each day do it this dramatically. Most people aren't torn away from their bodies, clinging to life. They die peacefully, already unconscious or asleep. Many people, of course, become very ill before they die. But most also have doctors, nurses and carers around to make sure they are comfortable and not suffering in their final days.

And while no one can predict exactly when this will happen to them, if you're young and healthy, the chances are that it'll be a long, long time yet.

The chances

Everybody dies of something, but for most people death is something that happens in old age and at the end of a long life. The most common causes of death are those linked to ageing bodies, with organs and systems that gradually grow weak and fail. Among these, the heart and circulatory system (the name for the vessels and tubes it pumps your blood through) are the most likely bits to finally give out.

In the developed world, for every 100 people who die, on average, around 57 will die peacefully in their sleep in old age – what's known as 'natural causes'. Another 20 will die of heart disease – as the heart stops pumping, or blood vessels become brittle or clogged up. Another 14 will die of cancer, as cells within organs and tissues start to grow too fast and the body loses the ability to hold them in check. And another 4 or 5 people will die of a stroke, which is when a blood vessel leading to the brain becomes blocked, and part of the brain it supplies becomes damaged through lack of oxygen.

All of these conditions happen most commonly to people well into old age. Now compare that with the remaining 4 in 100 who die sudden, early deaths from less natural causes (including everything from car accidents to fires, falls, drownings, shootings and lightning strikes). Look at it that way, and you see that your odds of reaching a ripe old age – and of dying a peaceful death, rather than a sudden, violent one – are very good. And if you look after yourself and your body, you can make the odds even better.

The lowdown

Death is not an evil curse, a contagious disease or a scary monster – it's a natural process that happens to our bodies just as it happens to the bodies of every plant, animal, mushroom and microbe on the planet. Just as leaves change and fall to feed the earth, so do our bodies and those of every other living creature. The earth, in turn, feeds the plants, which feed the animals, which feed on each other, and eventually cycle their nourishing nutrients back to the earth once more. Without death, there could be no life – so in a way we should be grateful for it.

If you've never experienced the death of someone close to you, death can seem scary because it's so mysterious and difficult to understand. Even if you have experienced this, it can still seem scary because it makes everybody feel so bad, and no one wants to talk about it.

When someone in your family (or even a much-loved pet) dies, it all seems so terrible because everyone is so sad. At funerals and burials, everyone is upset or crying. But this, too, is natural. We're sad that we won't get to be around them, to enjoy their company any more. We're sad, then, for ourselves rather than for the person or pet who has died, as they can't feel sad or lonely any more.

But once you've been through this, you eventually start to remember the person or pet as they were when they were alive, and you're happy and grateful for the time you got to share together. Although it can be very sad saying goodbye, you have the chance to understand death for what it is – neither good, nor bad, just a natural part of life itself.

Across the world, around 130,000 people die each day. But in the same day, 400,000 people are born. And so the cycle of life rolls on.

A near-death experience

In 1970, Kimberly Clark Sharp was out walking when she had a sudden heart attack and dropped dead on the pavement. Doctors later revived her, but while she was (technically) dead, she had what is known as a Near-Death Experience (NDE). Here's how she described it:

'I knew I was not alone, but I still couldn't see clearly, because I was enveloped in a dense, dark grey fog . . . Earthly time had no meaning for me any more. There was no concept of "before" or "after". Everything – past, present, future – existed simultaneously. Suddenly, an enormous explosion erupted beneath me, an explosion of light rolling out to the furthest limits of my vision. I was in the centre of the light. It blew away everything, including the fog. It reached the ends of the Universe, which I could see, and doubled back on itself in endless layers. I was watching eternity unfold.'

The fear

For some people, dying isn't such a scary idea. They're convinced that a better world awaits them on the other side, and they have a pretty good idea of what it might look like. But others are far less certain, and for them 'passing on' can be a terrifying thought, as they're fearful of what might or might not lie beyond. After all, there's more than one idea about what could happen . . .

Do we sleep forever, never to wake again? Or do we come back to life (or reincarnate) into the body of another person or animal? If so, who or what will it be? A king? A president? A dolphin? A dung beetle? If another world awaits us beyond this one, then where is it and what will it look like? Will our friends and families be there too, or will we never see them again? And what will *we* be like? Will our 'bodies' look the way they do during life? Or will they look older or younger? Will we have bodies at all? Will we recognize ourselves or others? Will we even remember who we were in our past lives? Think about it too much and it can all get a bit overwhelming.

The reality

Across the world, different peoples, cultures and religions have very different ideas of what may lie beyond our mortal lives. For many Hindus and Buddhists, it's rebirth into another body and another life here on Earth. For most Christians, Jews and Muslims, it's eternal life in another world far beyond and far different to ours – perhaps in another dimension or universe.

Japanese Shintoists walk a staircase to an afterworld with the spirits of their ancestors. Native American Indians pass on to the Happy Hunting Ground, where humans and animals live forever in eternal spring and summer. Some people believe there's nothing at all beyond this life – that we blink out like fireflies in the vast expanse of time and Space. Others believe we burn more brightly than ever after death – our energy joining with that of everyone and everything that has ever lived, and expanding to fill the entire Universe.

So who is right and who is wrong? What evidence do we have of what awaits us beyond death?

The truth is, we may never really know for sure, as (at least for now) science isn't equipped to deal with questions about other dimensions and universes, or to explain the mystery of where our consciousness (or 'thinking self') comes from, and where it might go after death.

Is there an afterworld in the sky above us? Well, no. We've journeyed into Space and orbited the planet, and we can see there isn't. Could it be somewhere else in Space – at the end of the Universe, perhaps? Possibly. But probably not. Because as far we know, there is no Space beyond the edge of our Universe. According to cosmologists, the Universe contains all the Space there is, so it's either bordered by nothingness, or it wraps around on itself and so has no edge at all! But could there be another world in another dimension, or even another universe? Maybe so. Cosmologists say that there are almost certainly more dimensions and universes beyond ours. Do we go there after death? Who knows? It's possible.

What about being reborn, or reincarnated, into another body? Well, we have no evidence for that beyond a few stories about children (or even animals) who can recognize people from their 'past lives', or people who say they can remember memories that aren't theirs. Could these stories be true? Possibly. Could the people involved be mistaken, or tricking themselves or others? That's possible, too. No biologist has ever *seen* a person or animal reincarnate. But in a way, all of us are 'reformed' into other bodies after death.

Our bodies decompose, and the atoms and molecules are recycled through soils, seas, microbes, plants, animals and people. Your body definitely contains at least a billion atoms that were once fish, cows, trees and lettuces. But since carbon atoms, especially, can circle the entire world in the seas and atmosphere, your body probably also contains at least a few carbon atoms that once belonged to Winston Churchill or King Henry VIII. You might even contain an atom or two of dinosaur! And just as the material of our bodies is conserved and recycled throughout the planet, so too is the energy contained within it. And what happens to our thoughts and memories after we die? Do they just disappear or do they go somewhere? And if so, do they migrate whole into new bodies, migrate into another dimension or universe, or just dissolve to join the energy of the known Universe? Who can say?

The lowdown

The point is, whatever 'the truth' about life after death may be, there's little sense being afraid of it just because we don't have all the answers. If you have strong religious beliefs then you probably aren't afraid, as you feel certain your idea of the afterlife is the right one. But even if you're not sure who's right and wrong, and you don't know what lies beyond, why be automatically afraid of it?

If you're afraid of something, that means you know (or you're guessing) it will be bad. But whether it's another body, another life, another universe, or just a rejoining with the matter and energy of this one, nothing we know suggests that what happens to us beyond our lives will be bad or scary. So if you don't know for sure, why not guess that it'll be good instead? Hey – it works for me!

In the end, a fear of what you don't or can't know is just a fear of *fear itself*. It's phobo-phobia. And where's the point, or the fun, in that?

So here we are at the end of our scary Fear Safari. We've seen almost every species of fear and phobia, and learned a lot of stuff along the way.

We found out that fear is both an emotion and a feeling. That emotions are physical changes that happen to the body. That feelings happen in the mind, partly in response to our emotions. And that by gaining a better understanding of our emotions, we can get better control of our feelings – including the feeling of fear.

We also discovered that some fears you're born with, while others you learn. The inborn fears evolved as part of a warning system, which helped our ancestors to survive in the past and still helps us to survive today. These include the fear of heights, darkness, drowning, snakes and sudden movement.

As for the 'learned' fears, they can develop in a number of different ways. We might learn them from experience, after a car crash or dog bite etches fear into our memories. More often, though, other people do the 'etching' for us, as friends, family, books, magazines, TV and movies can all create or exaggerate fears in our brains.

We found out why the feeling of fear builds and becomes worse with waiting, as anticipation leads to anxiety, dread and panic. We found out that most fears come from a lack of knowledge – a kind of automatic suspicion against the unknown or as-yet-unexplained. And perhaps most importantly of all, we discovered that exploring and explaining our fears are the first steps towards getting around them. Once fears become knowable and understandable, they're much easier to face. And if you want to face them, there are many ways to do it – both alone and with help from others.

It's been a crazy (and sometimes scary) ride, but I hope you felt it was worth it. If you now understand even a little bit more about the what, how and why of your fears, then I reckon it was!

The world can be a big, scary place. But knowing yourself and knowing where your fear comes from can help you face it all with courage and curiosity.

As a wise man once said, why be a chicken when you can be a tiger?

Or, at the very least, an extremely brave chicken.

Sources

1 Wild and Scary Wildlife

The hunter becomes the hunted
From 'Leopard Attack! A True Story of Survival in the African Bush' by John B. Snow. Article in *Outdoor Life* magazine, September 2006.

Fangs for the memory
Taken from 'I Should Be Dead' by Peter Jenkins. Article in www.venomousreptiles.org (Home of the Southeastern Hot Herp Society).

2 Natural Disasters

A very dodgy line
Eyewitness account taken from the National Ocean and Atmospheric Association's lightning safety page (http://www.lightningsafety.noaa.gov/story_missy.htm)

Hit by a twister
Eyewitness account taken from the Beecher Tornado Commemorative website (http://www.crh.noaa.gov/dtx/1953beecher/)

The wrath of Katrina
Statistics from the National Oceanic and Atmostpheric Administration's Hurricane Katrina page: www.katrina.noaa.gov/

Mount St Helens explodes
Account taken from Genzmer, Kershner & Schutz: *Great Disasters in History*. Parragon Books, 2007.

A 'second sun' falls on Siberia
From V. Vasiliev, A. F. Kovalevsky, S. A. Razin and L. E. Epiktetova: *Eyewitness accounts of Tunguska*. 1981.

3 Doctors, Dentists and Deadly Diseases

Needle nightmare
Author's own story, c.1990.

4 In the Unlikely Event

Smashed on the runway
Taken from Genzmer, Kershner & Schutz: *Great Disasters in History*. Parragon Books, 2007.

Tragedy strikes at sea
Taken from Genzmer, Kershner & Schutz: *Great Disasters in History*. Parragon Books, 2007.

The lane change he'll never forget
Personal account supplied by Paul Davey, used with permission.

5 In the Bad Place

Pitch-black panic
Author's own experience.

That sinking feeling
Excerpt from 'True Stories of Near Drowning' by Erik Henriksen. Article in *The Portland Mercury*, 15 July 2004.

Dizzy heights
From correspondence with the author, 2008. Reprinted with permission from Jake M., Wales.

Boxed in and up high? No way!
Submitted by the author's wife, 2008.

When the teacher picked me
From John R. Marshall and Suzanne Lipsett: *Social Phobia: From Shyness to Stage Fright*. Basic Books, 1995.

6 The Unknown

A near-death experience
Kimberly C. Sharp: *After the Light: What I Discovered on the Other Side of Life That Can Change Your World*. William Morrow, 1995.

Index

Why is SNOT green?

The First Science Museum Question and Answer Book

Glenn Murphy

Why is snot green? Do rabbits fart? What is space made of? Where does all the water go at low tide? Can animals talk? What are scabs for? Will computers ever be cleverer than people?

Discover the answers to these and an awful lot of other brilliant questions frequently asked at the Science Museum in this wonderfully funny and informative book.

How Loud Can You BURP?

and other extremely important questions (and answers) from the Science Museum

Glenn Murphy

How loud can you burp? Could we use animal poo in power stations to make electricity? Why is water wet, and is anything wetter than water? What's the deadliest disease in the world? What are clouds for?

A second volume of questions and answers from the Science Museum by the author of the mega-bestselling WHY IS SNOT GREEN? A wonderfully funny and informative book with loads of fascinating facts and no boring bits!

YOUR PLANET NEEDS YOU!

DAVE REAY

Illustrated by
ALAN ROWE

**Your planet needs you – so take action
before it's too late!**

**Join superhero Max and his friends Henry and Flora
as they become Global Warming Warriors, taking on
the Big Climate Culprits one by one. They'll give you
some top tips for fighting climate change – in your
kitchen, in your bedroom, at school, on holiday and in
the garden, and that's just for starters!**

A selected list of titles available from Macmillan Children's Books

The prices shown below are correct at the time of going to press. However, Macmillan Publishers reserves the right to show new retail prices on covers, which may differ from those previously advertised.

Why Is Snot Green?	978-0-330-44852-9	£4.99
Glenn Murphy		
How Loud Can You Burp?	978-0-330-45409-4	£4.99
Glenn Murphy		
Your Planet Needs You!	978-0-330-45095-9	£4.99
Dave Reay		

All Pan Macmillan titles can be ordered from our website, www.panmacmillan.com, or from your local bookshop and are also available by post from:

Bookpost, PO Box 29, Douglas, Isle of Man IM99 1BQ

Credit cards accepted. For details:
Telephone: 01624 677237
Fax: 01624 670923
Email: bookshop@enterprise.net
www.bookpost.co.uk

Free postage and packing in the United Kingdom